Reese Witherspoon

THE BIOGRAPHY

Reese Witherspoon

THE BIOGRAPHY

LAUREN BROWN

Thunder's Mouth Press
New York

REESE WITHERSPOON:
The Biography

Published by
Thunder's Mouth Press
An imprint of Avalon Publishing Group, Inc.
245 West 17th Street, 11th Floor
New York, NY 10011

AVALON
publishing group incorporated

Library of Congress Cataloging-in-Publication Data

Brown, Lauren, 1977-
Reese Witherspoon / by Lauren Brown.
p. cm.
Includes bibliographical references and index.
ISBN-13: 978-1-56025-988-6 (pbk. : alk. paper)
ISBN-10: 1-56025-988-4 (pbk. : alk. paper)
1. Witherspoon, Reese, 1976- 2. Motion picture actors and actresses--
United States--Biography. I. Title.
PN2287.W54B76 2007
791.43'028092--dc22
[B]
2007012547

Book design by Bettina Wilhelm

Printed in the United States of America
Distributed by Publishers Group West

Dedicated to:
Mom, Dad, Lindsie, and Marc, who never doubted me from beginning to
end

Le Sucre for their inspiration:
Steven, Alice, and Lauren

Lifelong friends for their motivation
Mindy, Michelle, Jessica, and Elissa

Jen Dienst for getting me to the finish line with her
amazing research skills

And Laura Jeanne Reese Witherspoon for sticking to her guns
and moving me to hold fast to mine

Contents

1

The Most Unusual Star in Hollywood

Britney Spears had a meltdown at age twenty-five, shaved her head, and went into rehab. Lindsay Lohan couldn't handle the party scene at age twenty and checked into rehab. Mary Kate Olsen, one-half of the famed child stars formerly known as the Olsen twins, finally succumbed to the pressure to be thin by Hollywood's deadly standards, and she, too, checked herself into a rehab facility for an eating disorder. All three girls soared to the spotlight at a young age, let their inhibitions go without taking any responsibility as they partied to the wee hours of the night, and hurt their images and even their careers as a result. It's become a rite of passage for these stars to be pictured in *Us* looking dazed, confused, and leaving a night of debauchery in the front seat of Paris Hilton's car.

Enter Reese Witherspoon. She's put together, she's classy, and she never lets her personal life affect her public persona, no matter what is happening in private. She doesn't put much stock into the whole see-and-be-seen mentality, as she told *Daily Express*. "A lot of people are defined by the parties they go to and the designers they wear. It must be exhausting, and a very easy trap to fall into. Whereas I am almost a hermit I stay in so much, but I really enjoy that." And she certainly does not understand young Hollywood today, which is ironic, since so many of those young actresses are desperate to have the same career trajectory as Reese's. "I grew up in a place where people just really want to go to work and go home to their kids and go to church on Sunday and just have a regular life, you know?" Reese told *Good Housekeeping*. "I'm the same way. I see people who are just becoming famous and I wonder, 'Which way are they going to go? Are they going to keep a head on their shoulders or totally lose their minds?' When people handle it well, it's wonderful. But sometimes . . ."

Reese is all of thirty-one, an Oscar-winning actress, and America's sweetheart. She was just as young as those girls when she started acting, but it took almost twelve years of her pounding the pavement to get on the cover of *People* magazine—and her cover was to celebrate her success, not to investigate a scandal. "I've strived my entire career to never be that person who is on every magazine cover at once. Or, you know, the toast of the town," Reese told *Bliss*. "It would be so much unbelievable pressure that I don't know how people deal with it."

Recently, Reese has been the center of attention as her seven-year marriage to the love of her life, actor Ryan Phillippe, ended in divorce. While other celebrities shack up with the first tattooed rock star they encounter or even their best friend's ex when their separations are final, Reese quietly carried on with her life, taking her kids to school, filming movies, and bringing her mom as her date to red carpet events like the Golden Globes. Many forget that Reese became pregnant at age twenty-three, before she was married to Ryan. This was before couples like Brad Pitt and Angelina Jolie made having a child before marriage (or without marriage at all) a socially acceptable and even trendy thing to do. How did she avoid scrutiny and negative press during that time? Like the mature and consummate professional Reese has been her entire life, she did not exploit her pregnancy, did not invite cameras into her home to get the first exclusive shots of her daughter, and married Ryan while she was still pregnant. She instantly eased into her two lives—her domestic life and her Hollywood life— and has never let the two cross paths since.

The birth of her second child went virtually unnoticed by the world. Instead, the focus was on her memorable and beloved movie roles such as perky sorority girl turned Harvard law student Elle Woods in *Legally Blonde*, or ambitious New York designer with a secret southern past in *Sweet Home Alabama*.

As Reese told *Premiere*: "I've been very calculated from the beginning about the career trajectory I want to have. Holly Hunter, Meryl Streep, Frances McDormand, Susan Sarandon—these are the women I want to emulate. I avoided the whole teen-movie thing because I want to be in this business for more than two years and I made conscious decisions not to do exploitative things because they don't feel right to me."

So, is it really possible in the age of being famous for simply being famous that Reese Witherspoon has managed to etch out a career based on her talent and adorable southern charm? When she won her Best Actress Oscar in 2006 for her portrayal of June Carter Cash in the Johnny Cash biopic *Walk the Line*, Reese famously quoted June while up at the podium: "I'm just trying to matter." That philosophy, of just trying to matter, and not trying to be the most talked-about star in Hollywood; just trying to do good work and live a good life, is what has made Reese stand out. Stars like Jessica Simpson have come out publicly to say that Reese's career is the one they most want to emulate. "I don't want a here-today, gone-tomorrow movie career," Jessica has said. "I want to be like Reese Witherspoon."

Reese, however, wants nothing to do with the careers stars like Simpson have built, based on playing up being dumb as an endearing quality. "Creating a cultural icon out of someone who goes, 'I'm stupid, isn't it cute?' makes me want to throw daggers. Saying that to young women, little girls . . . my daughter . . . is not OK," Reese has said. "I want to say [to those stars], my grandma did not fight for what she fought for, my mother did not fight for what she fought for, just so you can start telling women it's fun to be stupid."

Reese has been consistent with her morals and values. She has her feet planted firmly on the ground and doesn't buy into the competitive and cutthroat culture of Hollywood. "I figured out I'm never going to be the 'most' anything," Reese told CosmoGIRL! "I'm never going to be the richest person in the world. I'm never going to be the skinniest actress in Hollywood. I'm never going to be the smartest person I've ever met. I'm never going to be the funniest person. But I can work extremely hard to be the best person I can be."

Reese never rebelled or acted out or went through a phase of hard partying followed by a period of sainthood to try and abolish a bad reputation. Her idea of a good time isn't an all-weekend party spree in a hot city like Las Vegas or Miami. No, Reese gets her kicks with a trip to the Container Store. "Cleaning out a drawer makes me feel calm and sorted," Reese told Vanity Fair. "I remember organizing my toys when I was seven years old and my bookshelves, too."

Reese is a rare breed. She is one of the only actresses out there that young fans can look up to and aspire to be like, with so many others doing drugs, sleeping around, and missing work because they're too hungover to crawl out of bed for their call time. The truth of the matter is that when Reese takes off her designer dresses after a night on the red carpet, or washes the makeup off her face after a long day

of filming, she instantly reverts back to a little girl from Nashville, Tennessee. "Someone [from back home] will always say to me, *You're* a
movie star? Why did this happen to you?' I'll say, 'I have absolutely no
idea why this happened to me!'" Reese explained to the *Chicago Sun-
Times*. "And my old friends will gather around me and say, 'But it's *you*!
Of all people, why *you*?' And I'll repeat, 'You got me!'" But anyone
who has been following Reese's career since her first starring role at
age fourteen in the poignant *The Man in the Moon* knows why. She's
real. She's the girl you want on your side and want giving you advice.
With her, what you see is what you get. And being an actress is just the
beginning of what Reese wants to be known for in her lifetime. "I
don't think this is the end of what I'm supposed to accomplish. I think
it's just leading me to some path I haven't found yet. All the attention
actors get—it's so unmerited. It's so insignificant, what I've done,"
Reese told *Vanity Fair*. "My parents devoted their lives to taking care of
people, and they couldn't enumerate all the lives they've saved. I want
to carry on the legacy of caring and compassion. I feel strongly about
the lack of health care in America, and I really want to help people.
This is not the end of it."

Welcome to the life of Reese Witherspoon. She's the star who has
no idea how famous she is and would be OK if everything ended
tomorrow. Reese has dreams, goals, and opinions that no other star of
her age and stature can match.

2

The Makings of a Star

Fame wasn't necessarily the goal for thirteen-year-old Reese Witherspoon as she stood in line with half her hometown of Nashville, Tennessee. What were they waiting for? The chance to audition for a bit
part in *The Man in the Moon*—a big Hollywood movie that was filming
in town. Her friend saw a notice in the local newspaper advertising a
casting call for extras, and Reese decided to tag along.

It wasn't a total stretch that Reese was there—in fact, it would
have been more of a surprise if she'd let this opportunity pass her by.
Reese was a minisuperstar in Nashville. She'd been acting circles
around the rest of the town since she was just a little girl. It all started
when Reese was just seven years old and booked her very first commercial. "There was a little girl who lived down the street and her parents owned a flower shop. They asked me to be in their local
commercial, and I was just bit," Reese recalled to *Vanity Fair*. "I came
home and told my mother I wanted to be an actress. It all came from
me. It was all self-generated." From there she went on to model in
the Sunday paper—kids' track suits and other fashions—as well as
star in other local commercials. Reese also started entering talent

competitions, and when she was eleven years old she won the "Ten-State Talent" award.

But Reese's parents figured that filming commercials and modeling were just other after-school activities, along with gymnastics, cheerleading, and Girl Scouts. Reese was an organized and diligent child. Everything had to have its order, and everything she did was done with the highest of standards. Instead of a pet name like "Sweetheart" or "Pumpkin," which most children receive from their parents . . . Reese's parents couldn't find anything more fitting than "Little Miss Type A." It was a name that Reese lived up to and that her parents took seriously. So even though Reese enjoyed acting and was pretty good at it, too, her parents expected their "Little Miss Type A" to follow in their footsteps and find a career in the field of medicine.

Ever the overachiever, Reese read levels ahead of her peers in kindergarten and toyed with becoming either an OB/GYN or the first president of the United States during a presentation in front of her class in the third grade. Yet acting became a priority for Reese, and even though she tried to fight it and tried not to make a big deal of it, it was her passion. Not only was it her passion, but it was her God-given, natural-born talent. At just seven years old, Reese enrolled in children's acting classes. By the time she was nine, she was in the adult program acting out scenes and holding her own with other students three times her age. "I was a very empathetic child. I was always studying people and their dialects. I would try to imitate the way they spoke," Reese told the *Mail on Sunday*. And Reese's parents never wanted to deter Reese from her dreams— even if they were different from their own. "I wanted to be an actor when I was seven years old, and my parents thought it was a very strange choice for a little girl in Tennessee. But they were always really cool about it, and if it was something I wanted to do, they would drive me to the lessons," she says. "I always really appreciated that, because you don't ever feel like your dreams are stupid. I had a man on a plane once turn to me, and he was talking about his kid and how he didn't want to take her to ice skating lessons—he said they're too expensive. He was sitting in *first class* and was like, 'I can't pay for my kid's ice skating lessons.' I said, 'You know, I'm so glad I didn't have a parent like you.' My [parents] are, like, the most proud people . . . and they've always reveled in my success because they were very open-minded."

So as fourteen-year-old Reese stood in line to vie to be an extra in *The Man in the Moon*, she was bursting with excitement—but only on the inside. Sure, she was trying to play it cool, but that was typical of Reese. She never wanted to put too much stock in something that wasn't a sure thing, and she certainly wasn't going to get ahead of herself at a casting call to be an extra! Reese was a private child. She kept to herself and had dreams, ideas, and thoughts that she didn't share with others but took great pride in when she was alone and day-dreaming. "I like attention," an adult Reese admitted. And Reese as a child already knew this, before her acting career came to be. She may have told herself and her parents that acting was just a hobby, but she knew it was something bigger—it was her destiny.

Laura Jeanne Reese Witherspoon was born in New Orleans, Louisiana, to John, a military surgeon, and Betty, a registered nurse. She has an older brother, John. Young Reese spent the first four years of her life on an Army base in Wiesbaden, Germany—worlds away from the glitz and glamour of Hollywood—while her father was a lieutenant colonel in the reserves and fulfilled his draft obligation from the Vietnam War.

Overachieving runs deep in the veins of Reese's heritage. She's a direct descendant of John Witherspoon, a signer of the Declaration of

Independence who was also president of Princeton University. "My dad's an ear, nose, and throat surgeon. He works extremely hard. And my mom's a pediatric nurse who is completely driven," Reese told *Reader's Digest*. "She has six degrees, and she taught me about taking care of yourself and that it's important to have a sense of independence. She was a great example of being self-made."

Reese's family moved back to the United States when she was four and they settled into the southern comfort of a slow-paced life in Nashville, Tennessee, where her family had a long and vast history. "Nashville is where my family is from, so it was nice that we had a heritage there. I got to spend a lot of time with my grandparents before they passed away, so that was an invaluable experience for me," Reese told *Teen People*. "Nashville is beautiful. It's one of those places where you really know what people are like. Southern is a personality type. I enjoy being southern." Reese held strong to her southern roots and even came out twice as a debutante—big white dress and all. "It's more something you do out of tradition and respect for your family, rather than something you do to get a husband like it used to be."

Reese enjoyed the traditional southern upbringing and never questioned some of the rules that were imposed on her as a result. "The way I was brought up, I wasn't allowed to wear black and I wasn't allowed to wear bikinis. And I was only allowed to wear two shades of lipstick—peach or pink. It was all about what was 'appropriate,'" Reese explained to *Vanity Fair*. "The South is a lot of traditions and a lot of manners. The only joke my mother knows is: 'Why do southern women make bad prostitutes? Because they have to write too many thank-you notes.'"

Those who knew Reese when she was young probably would not have pegged her as Hollywood's future "it" girl. She was a shy and awkward little girl with Coke-bottle glasses. She was always the smallest in her class and didn't have many friends.

But what many probably did not know was that Reese was "acting" on the playground in an effort to overcome her shyness and insecurities and make some friends. She started to pretend she was a different character each day to get over her social anxiety, while entertaining her peers at the same time. "I decided one day I was going to be the 'grandma from Texas,' and suddenly I had friends, and I'd never had friends before," Reese told *Marie Claire*. "It was just a thing I discovered: if you're able to make fun of yourself, people are attracted to you that much more."

Reese's parents thought she was hysterical, which definitely built her confidence. "My mother is very funny and laughs all the time. And she made me feel funny, because everything I ever said was funny to her," Reese told *Reader's Digest*. "I was always doing impressions. I remember I used to do this whole routine where I would answer my telephone with different accents, and my mother and father thought it was hysterical." For the most part, however, Reese was private and quiet despite being full of imagination. She adored her older brother, John, and spent a lot of time with him. "We weren't the kind of children that were shadowed. We didn't have nannies. We didn't have housekeepers," she told *Interview*. "I was alone a lot but it was probably self-imposed, because I really loved privacy!"

About one month after Reese stood in line with practically all of Nashville, Tennessee, in an attempt to land a chance to be an extra in *The Man in the Moon*, she went out to get the mail and found something that would change her life forever. Waiting for her was a package from Hollywood. It turned out that Reese was not going to be needed as an extra for *The Man in the Moon*, after all. Instead, the producers had sent

her the script for the movie, because they wanted her to take a slightly
larger role—the lead, to be exact. As fourteen-year-old Reese stood
in her driveway holding the script in her hand, she knew that she was
no longer going to be just another kid in the hall at school. She was
going to have to convince her parents that this was the path she wanted
to take, and she was going to have to balance schoolwork with learning
her lines and traveling as far away as Los Angeles. "My parents were
deeply confused as to why I wanted to do this," Reese told *Jane*. "But
they were shockingly supportive."

Reese went for a screen test for the movie and did land the lead. It
was at that moment that she had to sit down with her parents and seriously discuss if acting was something they were going to let her do.
They decided she would do the one movie, see how it went, and if it
ended up being a success, they would go from there. "I never really
decided to be an actor. It all just happened for me. Like out of
nowhere. It was really bizarre," Reese recalled to *Star Talk* about the
experience. "Everyone said it was so 'Lana Turner' the way it happened
for me. I always felt like this career chose me and I did not choose it."

It was an emotional movie and character that Reese had booked for
her first foray into Hollywood.

The Man in the Moon was about a precocious fourteen-year-old girl
named Dani (that was Reese's role) who falls in love with her seventeen-
year-old neighbor in rural Louisiana in the '50s. It was a role that
required an emotional depth that Reese herself hadn't yet experienced. But she went into it like a pro, and her costars, which included
some seasoned actors such as Sam Waterston and Tess Harper, started
calling Reese by the nickname "Little Meryl." The Meryl they were
referring to, of course, was the legendary and Oscar-winning actress
Meryl Streep. Life was turned upside down as Reese started assimilating

herself into "Hollywood" now that she was in a major motion picture. She needed to hire managers, publicists, and agents to work with her on *The Man in the Moon*, and attempt to keep her career going after she was finished with it. She hired Steve Dontanville from the William Morris Agency to be her agent. He flew to Nashville to meet Reese and her parents, and he was taken aback by the way Reese at only fourteen years old was grilling him with questions about how he was going to handle her career and make sure she was treated fairly. At that point, the biggest acting jobs Reese had booked were regional commercials for local attractions like Opryland, but she was calling the shots at their meeting like she had been landing starring roles in movies for years. "She was this very opinionated, focused person— very powerful and self-assured—a little southern spitfire," Dontanville remembered about their first encounter to *Vanity Fair*. "But she was this riveting, beautiful girl who just jumped off the screen. She was just natural."

Reese reflected years later to *Vanity Fair* that maybe she had been a little too opinionated as an unknown teenager just breaking into Hollywood. "They want people they can push around," Reese said. "I was the girl who was always asking, 'Why? Yeah, I know you want me to do that, but why?' I always thought people wanted to hear my opinions. It's only as I've become older that I realized no one wants to hear my opinions. But I'd give them anyway. It's just blind self-confidence. I get like a little terrier about things. My mom said I should have been an attorney."

It was meeting people like Dontanville, however—who truly did want to hear and honor Reese's opinions, and believed that she had a real talent that could take her far—that helped ease the fears that Reese's parents had about her decision to make the movie and hopefully continue acting. "In the beginning my parents didn't really understand what moviemaking was all about, and they didn't want me to fall into a nefarious career," Reese recalled to the *Mail on Sunday* in London. "They were worried that it might be seedy. They had wanted me to be a physician or surgeon, but in the end I couldn't have asked for more supportive parents."

Reese went back to Nashville after filming wrapped, and everything went back to exactly the way it had been before. Reese kept on auditioning, but since none of her work had hit movie theaters yet, no one really knew what she had been doing and where she had been. Flying under the radar as Nashville's newest actress, however, ended almost a year later on October 4, 1991, when *The Man in the Moon* opened in theaters. The reviews for Reese were glowing. According to Janet Maslin's review in the *New York Times*, "Miss Witherspoon has no trouble carrying a lot of the film single-handedly." Now she just had to go back to school and try to fit in with the rest of her peers.

A star had officially been born, and Reese was only a sophomore in high school. With her parents' support, she kept on going, and scripts started pouring in. She made a few made-for-TV movies and had roles in a few more wide-release movies, but nothing that was making her a household name—yet. And Reese was extremely humbled by all the attention and opportunities that were coming her way. Nothing was going to her head, as was proven when she had the opportunity to audition for the lead in the movie *Cape Fear*. Martin Scorsese was directing and Robert De Niro was the star. Even though they were perhaps two of the most notable, famous, and legendary people in Hollywood, Reese was too young at the time to fully understand who they were or just how powerful they were. So she was blissfully ignorant on the plane to Los Angeles to meet with both Martin *and* Robert about the role. That was, until she began conversing with another passenger on her flight. When she said who she was going to be meeting with and why, the passenger started going on about how significant and notorious they were, and Reese became incredibly and inconsolably nervous. She was so out of sorts by the time she got to the audition that she completely blew it. The role ultimately went to Juliette Lewis.

It didn't stop her from trying to find bigger and better roles, and Reese hoped her classmates would show the same unwavering support as her family. "When you have an extraordinary job like making movies and I was living in Nashville and everybody there was just sort of having a normal life. When you're fourteen, I think you desperately just want to be like everyone else," Reese told *TNT*. "I was just constantly trying to acclimate and trying to be like everyone else so people didn't feel like I was better than everybody else [for making movies]."

3

High School with Hollywood for Homework

High school for Reese was challenging, because everyone knew that she was a budding movie star. Even though she tried to arrange her schedule to film during the summer, she still found herself trying to do whatever she could to not stick out, since everyone knew who she was and what she was doing when she was missing school for extended periods of time. "It took me four years to make friends, maybe because there were preconceived notions about who I was. I think a lot of people go through that," Reese told *CosmoGIRL!* "I've learned it's not important to have fifty million friends; it's important to have just one or two that you can tell *anything* to. There was a time early on in high school where there was a lot of pressure to be mean. You were cool if you were mean-spirited to other people. I think that's so uncool now. You do it because you're so completely insecure about yourself that you can't be cool about other people."

Reese attended the famed and prestigious Harpeth Hall preparatory school in Nashville. It was a private, all-girls school with other famous alumni like the Grand Ole Opry's Minnie Pearl and Grammy-award-winning singer Amy Grant. Reese loved everything about her high school. "I loved my uniform, loved not having to compete for male attention, loved that we were able to focus on our work, loved not having the drama of relationships in high school—and it's not like we missed out on that stuff. We had plenty of it on the weekends," Reese explained to the *New York Daily News*.

The drama that Reese tried hard to avoid was from other students who were envious of her acting career. She became a cheerleader—a very uncharacteristic move on her part—just so she could seem "normal" on campus. "I had big glasses and my vision was so bad I couldn't see the E on the eye chart. I certainly wasn't the homecoming queen or the prettiest girl in school. I was a big dork who read a lot of books, but I was a popular dork because I learned to be funny," is how Reese describes herself in high school.

The students and teachers that she did connect with were extremely supportive of her acting career. "Being at an all-girls high school, I made some of the best friends of my life because there was such camaraderie and I had never had a sister, so I have, like, eight sisters now," Reese recalled about high school to *Teen People*. "I had great teachers who really inspired me to do great things and move to great cities and make lots of money! I had a great English teacher who really inspired me in my junior year in high school. I developed such a passion for reading and studying material that has been so helpful for me in this business." Her passion for language didn't go unnoticed—her high school nickname was "Big Words." But high school for Reese— despite her acting career—seemed to stay normal. Case in point: she had a huge crush on Jim Morrison, the deceased lead singer of the Doors. "My girlfriend and I went to see the Doors movie six times. I had a six-foot poster of him on my ceiling. I was obsessed," she remembers.

Her friends would come over and pick out one of her dad's vintage Cadillacs from his collection to ride around town in. "They were like big boats," Reese told *Teen People*. "We used to call them the 'hooptie rides!'" Even though she attended an all-girls school, Reese was still able to meet boys and date. "I was always in a serious relationship," Reese told *Teen People*. "I liked going to an all-girls school because boyfriends and relationships can be very distracting from school. It was really nice to have that part of my life be separate from the school experience—even though I definitely had drama with the boys!" That drama even included a prom date who wasn't so keen on the details of the evening—like what time to pick Reese up! "Senior prom was a weird situation. I went to an all-girls high school, so I had to do the asking. I asked this boy who was a junior. Everyone was supposed to meet at my house—and he didn't show up. It was getting later and later and later, and finally my *dad* put on his tux and was ready to take me," Reese told *CosmoGIRL!* "Then the guy shows up, like, 'Oh, sorry.' Like it was no big deal. It was my *senior prom*! I ended up going with him, but he officially lost his name. For the rest of my senior year, we just called him 'Prom Date.' My friends even made these pins that had his face on them, with the words I LOVE PROM DATE!"

But being a movie star did give Reese a sense of independence that she hadn't experienced before—especially when it came to her parents and things like curfews that they wanted to impose on her. "I had this newfound independence and I couldn't believe that my mother was asking me to come home at one in the morning on prom night," Reese recalled to *Seventeen*. "I was like, 'I don't think so! I'm staying out all night long and I'm not coming in—period!'" That attitude, however, was not something that Reese's parents were going to tolerate if she were to continue her acting career. "I had a family who taught me that life isn't just about you: it's about family and friends and giving back," Reese explained to *Good Housekeeping*. "I mean, I know there were moments when people around me might have been fearful that because of fame or celebrity, I was going to go off the rails, but that was never an option. I really attribute that to my family—they keep it all in perspective." And Reese had promised her parents she wouldn't let it all go to her head and that she would never disrespect her family. "I didn't want to rebel. My brother was very rebellious, and I promised my mother I wouldn't be a rebellious teenager," Reese told *Vanity Fair*. Besides, being away for acting gigs all the time made it easier for Reese to behave. "I never went through that period where I hated my family. I was always away so much I never really had to hate them," she told *Seventeen*.

That was a good thing, because Reese needed her family's support and commitment to her decisions. Being a southern girl in Hollywood was not always easy—even for someone as driven and motivated as Reese. "I always felt like people didn't understand me, what I was capable of or what I could accomplish. I was driven to make people understand that I was capable of more," Reese told *Daily Express* in the UK. "People would assume [because I had a southern accent] that I was not educated or ignorant or that I was married to my cousin. My agent told me that if I didn't lose the accent I would never work again."

4

Big Actress on Campus

In the spring of 1994, when Reese graduated at the top of her class from Harpeth Hall, she had made a total of six movies besides *The Man in the Moon*. She could very easily have bypassed college and headed straight for Hollywood, as the movies and scripts were pouring in. But her parents insisted that she at least try higher education. Education was an integral part of their lives—John, her father, had scored a perfect 1600 on his SATs. Plus there was a part of John and Betty that hoped Reese would get so caught up in college life that she would decide to devote her time to earning a degree in medicine and leave acting behind. Even though Reese knew that she was sure about acting, she didn't want to disappoint her parents. Despite completing so much of her high school schoolwork on movie sets, Reese had still excelled at all of her classes and could basically have gotten in to any school her heart desired, but she decided to attend the prestigious Stanford University in Palo Alto, California. Reese was still making movies; had movies she'd already made still due to come out in theaters; and was entertaining offers for future movies. She wasn't exactly sure how she was going to balance Hollywood with schoolwork. This was

"Little Miss Type A," however, so Reese knew she could figure out some sort of arrangement to get it all done. In the fall of 1994, Reese and her parents packed her things in the family car and started driving across the country to Stanford. It was then that Reese had her first moment of doubt and panic about going away to school. "I told my mom to forget the whole thing and turn the car around," she told *Seventeen*. "For years I had been going off for three months at a time to make movies and it was no big deal. Then suddenly I'm on my way to Stanford, I totally regress into this child. I was terrified I wouldn't have any friends."

The fall of 1994 at Stanford created a lot of buzz on campus. It had a unique tagline. It was the "Celebrity Class," because, in addition to Reese, stars such as *Wonder Years* actor Fred Savage, golf prodigy Tiger Woods, and Olympic gymnast Dominique Dawes were all incoming freshmen. It was comforting to Reese that she wasn't the only famous face on campus, and she hoped it would take some of the attention away from her—though she says today that the only celebrity she ever actually saw was Savage. At this point in Reese's career, she was a known star, but she hadn't yet made a hugely successful movie that would garner the mass frenzy that peers like Alicia Silverstone (to whom Reese was often compared, as well as mistaken for) garnered, so Reese was hopeful she would blend in on campus like everyone else.

Reese actually drew a lot more attention than she could ever have anticipated. It just didn't occur to Reese that most of the movies she had made up to that point in her career—starting with *The Man in the Moon* and ending with her latest film, *S.F.W.*—had been geared to an audience of her own age group. *S.F.W.* was probably the movie that she was recognized the most for on campus, as it was a take on how gullible the MTV generation had become. Reese played Wendy Pfister, who is

one of five hostages held inside a convenience store for thirty-six days.
The terrorists' only demand is that the whole ordeal be televised live
and uncut—or everyone will die. Stephen Dorff, who was best known
for a TV movie called *I Know My First Name Is Steven*, played Cliff Spab,
a hostage whose wit, humor, and catchphrase "So fucking what?" capture the audience's attention and turn him into a media superstar.
Reese's take on *S.F.W.* was that "it's a parody on how the American
media makes less-than-average people into national heroes. These kids
in the film are not profound, but the media turns them into idiot
savants and feeds the public lies and fabrications, which it swallows
completely, especially my generation," she told *Interview*. While *S.F.W.*
wasn't a huge blockbuster, it made an impact on those who did see it
and had a cult following among its young fans. Reese learned this as
soon as she hit the Stanford campus. "Everyone was really enamored
of *S.F.W.*, which amused me," she says. "This guy once stopped me in
the hall and said, 'Oh, my God, you're Wendy Pfister!' and I said,
'Who?' I didn't even remember the name. He's like, 'You're Wendy
Pfister!' And I was like, 'Oh, my God, from *S.F.W.*? I can't believe you
saw that movie.'" *S.F.W.* wasn't the only movie that was getting her recognized on campus. "I had never been in a place where that group was
so concentrated," she told *Seventeen*. "Everybody on campus knew me
by different characters, which surprised me." But there were those
students who weren't such big fans of Reese and who assumed she was
getting special treatment and privileges because she was a star. They
gave her a hard time. "I think there was sort of a prejudice against me
being an actress. I mean, I think a lot of people thought I got in just
because I was a star," Reese told *Star Interviews*. "And I applied just the
same way everybody else did. You know, under my real name that
nobody recognizes me under."

Reese was able to ignore those misled classmates and, before long, had assimilated herself into college life and blended in on campus. She declared her major as English literature and "Little Miss Type A" had no trouble keeping up with her demanding course load. "I was a pretty good student," Reese told Hollywood.com of her college days. "[But] I was always busy on some sort of tangent and thinking about other things, not what was at hand, so I was kind of a last-minute kind of person. But I loved writing papers . . . researching and being in the library . . . I loved that stuff."

While Reese was writing papers and attending classes, she was still doing all she could to keep her career going. She would be down the hall and someone would yell for her to get back to her room because a director like Oliver Stone was on the phone to discuss a project he had in mind for Reese, or her publicist had the latest update on her press commitments. It was surreal for her fellow residents in the on-campus Cedro House, where she lived.

Reese's roommate was her unofficial personal secretary. "She's like, 'OK, Reese—yesterday your agent called and then your publicist and you're going to be doing a photo shoot.' I can't even imagine being the roommate of some girl who was an actress, but she was really cool about it," Reese recalled to *Seventeen*.

Reese's roommate may have been her unofficial secretary, but she made a hallmate by the name of Liz McDade-Montez her official assistant when she went to Minnesota in the middle of her winter quarter to make the comedy *Overnight Delivery*. The movie costarred Paul Rudd, who at that time had just become a star from his turn in the hit movie *Clueless*. In *Overnight Delivery*, Rudd played Wyatt, a student at the University of Minnesota who is convinced his girlfriend back home is cheating on him. After writing her a letter to tell her that it's over, he discovers he was wrong about the whole thing and must get that letter. So with the help of his friend Ivy, played by Reese, they go on a road trip in an attempt to intercept the letter before it's too late.

Reese was thrilled to have the bonus of having her friend join her on the set and take on the duties of her personal assistant. Liz wasn't worried about missing a quarter of school because she knew this was the opportunity of a lifetime. She had the support of her family and friends back home, but her friends at Stanford were skeptical. Even though Reese had found her niche on campus, there were still students who wondered about her commitment to Stanford since she was still making movies. In actuality, they were envious, but neither Reese nor Liz let it affect them. Liz even got to appear in the movie as an extra! "[I wanted] to take advantage of this opportunity. It was a one-time thing. I don't plan on being a personal assistant forever," she told the *Stanford Daily*.

Since Reese was using the money she earned from making movies to pay her college tuition, she found it very hard to turn movie roles down. "It's hard because, am I going to have a high-paying career or go to school and do the right thing?" she told the *Stanford Daily*. "Everybody [on campus] got used to my lifestyle. Stanford is good for actors because it's big enough for you to have your own life," she said. After she wrapped *Overnight Delivery*, Reese was getting ready to settle back into college life and really start focusing on her studies. But before she got too comfortable, she got a call from director Oliver Stone with an offer that she couldn't refuse. He was producing a dark, edgy twist on the Little Red Riding Hood fable called *Freeway* starring Kiefer Sutherland. Reese was to play Vanessa Lutz, a trashy, tough-talking fifteen-year-old with a barely-there wardrobe. After her parents are both put in jail *again*, Vanessa decides to go search for the grandmother she never knew instead of being put in another foster home. "On the way to Grand-mother's house" Vanessa's car breaks down, and she's picked up from the side of the road by Bob Wolverton, a counselor at a school for trou-bled boys. After they earn each other's trust, Vanessa realizes that he's actually "The I-5 Killer" from the news and desperately tries to escape.

When Reese met with Oliver Stone about the role of Vanessa, she took the meeting completely in character. "I walked in there chewing gum and was just like, 'Yeah—so do you want me to do this role or what?'" Reese recalled on an interview on *E!* "That was the character, so I wasn't going to walk in there and be like, 'Please, Mr. Stone, please hire me' and bat my eyelashes at him." Despite being so ballsy during her meeting, deep down she was terrified of taking on a role so completely different from anything she had done before. "When I got the script, I thought, 'This scares me half to death, I have to see if I can do it.'" The script was challenging in itself. "I had to say things I never said before in my whole life. Being southern, there are just cer-tain things you don't talk about," Reese told *Seventeen*. Reese, however, ultimately embraced the role, accepted the challenge, immersed her-self in the part, and analyzed the character so she could really under-stand her. "I don't see Vanessa as being bad. I see her as sort of a person who's always seeking the truth. And is that a bad thing? I mean, she was always searching out honesty and wanting people to be as honest as she was with them. I mean, the first person she sees she tells them about her sexual experience with her father and, you know, how her mother was in prison, and this is a person who lives her life freely and in an honest way," Reese explained to TNT's *Rough Cut*. "I think there's nothing more admirable than somebody who aspires to those sorts of things. And I don't think she's a bad girl. I mean, yeah, she shoots people in the head, but that's the spirit of the movie."

But when Reese's prim and proper southern mother came to the set, she almost had a heart attack watching her daughter prance around in a tiny tube top and leather ensemble. It was the one and only time that Reese questioned taking the part. "My mother watched me solicit myself. She's like—'I don't know, Reese, are you sure this is what you want to do for a living?'" If anything, the experience of making *Freeway* further cemented Reese's desire to be an actress and made her rethink her path as a student at Stanford. "That's when I finally totally got what acting was about—dissolving into my work rather than being conscious of myself and how I looked," Reese told *Cosmopolitan*. The challenge of playing such a violent, aggressive, and angry character gave Reese a sense of satisfaction she had never imagined. "I realized then that acting is what I wanted to do with my life," Reese told *Mr. Showbiz*. "Up until that point, frankly, I wasn't challenging myself. I got the script for *Freeway* and it scared me half to death. I thought, 'I should try this and if not I'll go back to school and be a doctor.'"

Her performance was universally lauded and put her on every producer and director's wish list of young actresses they wanted to work with. Reese was relieved. "I was scared to death of that role," she says. "Because I knew that I could take a chance, and it would either work or everybody would say, 'Oh, my God, what was she thinking?!'" And while she loved getting such praise and acclaim, Reese didn't let it go to her head. Instead, it just challenged her to keep doing bigger and better and to work even harder. "From then on, I was just like, 'I'm never going to skate through again. This is what I was meant to do.' I have really overachiever parents," she says, "who push me to go beyond what people think of me, and I was just skating by. I was like, 'If I'm not going to challenge myself, I don't deserve to be here.'"

When *Freeway* hit theaters, it wasn't exactly box office gold, but it did for Reese's career exactly what she hoped it would. "Now they don't always think, 'Oh, she's just a nice southern girl,'" Reese told *Seventeen*. "People want to see actors push themselves and do things they wouldn't do, and for a long time I played it really safe. I'm not so scared anymore."

Reese stayed true to that philosophy, and the next role that she was offered was a supporting role in a movie called *Twilight*, with Paul Newman and Susan Sarandon. The movie was significant to Reese for many reasons. For one, it would feature her first topless scene. Since it wasn't going to be done in a distasteful or exploitive way, she was completely comfortable with filming such a scene from the moment she took the part. She described her topless scene as inconsequential yet necessary to the film. Second, it would be a chance for Reese to work with icons like Paul Newman and Susan Sarandon, whom she looked up to immensely. "I got to stand next to Paul Newman. I've seen practically everything he's ever done—it was such a wonderful fantasy and also to have that person live up to every expectation that you have of him," Reese said of the experience. "And even further beyond that, he inspired me to do the right things with celebrity and fame."

The most significant thing that came out of Reese accepting the role in *Twilight* was that it forced her to make the decision to leave Stanford indefinitely. If Reese was going to really focus on her career and keep nabbing high-profile roles, she was going to have to move to Los Angeles full-time and focus only on making movies. "Hollywood eats you alive," Reese told *Seventeen*. "I'm one of those highly organized people who like to have everything meticulously in place. Now it's too hard to plan a dentist appointment, much less plan three months ahead to enroll in classes." So, Reese withdrew from Stanford and moved to

Los Angeles without looking back. "I probably wouldn't have pursued acting if it had not fallen in my lap like it did. If I had had to move to L.A. and live in my car, I would not have acted. It's not practical enough," says Reese. "My parents wanted me to stay in school, and I do miss the structure of school. It helped me learn about other people's ideas and be analytical about things. But I don't regret [dropping out of Stanford]. It's over."

5
Pleasantville

With Stanford behind her, Reese was ready to give herself completely to Hollywood. She moved all her belongings from her dorm at Stanford to a cozy apartment in Los Angeles. She maintained a low profile, as she wasn't hugely recognizable just yet. "I'm *huge* with parking lot attendants. Huge!" Reese told *Seventeen*. "I've done enough films so people feel like I'm their own private secret. They say, 'I saw that movie! *Nobody* else saw that movie!'"

At first, being all alone was too much for Reese, and she would constantly call her mom, dad, and brother back home in Nashville just so she could hear familiar and comforting voices. "I don't feel like I have a home here," Reese told *Seventeen*. "It's sad sometimes, like on Thanksgiving when you can't go back because it's such a short holiday. It's a weird time, your early twenties when you're really individual and alone but not ready to start your own family." Reese did make one good girlfriend—a neighbor in her apartment building named Heather, with whom she's still friends to this day. "I walked over and knocked on her door because I didn't know anybody and said, 'Will you please come have coffee with me? I don't have any friends,'" Reese told *Harper's Bazaar*. "She said, 'I don't have any friends either.'" Of course, it wasn't long before Reese had movies to make that kept her so busy she didn't have time to miss anyone—or make more friends!

The first that came her way was a look at American life in the fifties versus the nineties called *Pleasantville*. It was a unique concept in that half the movie took place in color and half in black and white, and Reese was very excited about what the film commented on socially. "We all think of the fifties in one particular way. That's sort of how the early way you see *Pleasantville* is sort of perceived as—this perfect, idyllic setting with picket fences and beautiful houses and nice, white families. But as the movie progresses, you start to see this undercurrent of everything that was underneath the fifties," Reese told *Entertainment Tonight*. "Especially fifties' television turmoil and hate and discomfort and distress, and I think people will really be talking about how this movie sort of represents the juxtaposition between what was on television in the fifties and what was really happening in the fifties."

The film was directed by first-time director Gary Ross, who was better known for writing scripts like the Tom Hanks comedy *Big*. Reese was extremely impressed with Gary as they began working together. "At first I was really struck by Gary Ross's writing. I had no idea what he would be like as a director. There was no work to look at. But as a writer he completely embodied the voice of '90s teenagers, '50s teenagers, all these different voices. Every character is so distinct and wonderfully mature. He found a character arc for everyone that was so appealing," Reese told *Star Talk*. "For actors, there's nothing better than working with a director who has as great a part as you do, and you can all contribute in different ways. When we went into the rehearsal process I remember being stuck on a scene and I couldn't figure out what I was supposed to be saying. I said to Gary,

'I don't know what I'm saying here,' and he took me through the scene. He said, 'This is what you're saying, but this is what you really mean,' and he told us the subtext of every line in the entire scene. For a writer to be that in touch with what he is trying to say, he's just very conscious of everything all along the way."

Reese was to costar alongside Oscar-nominated actress Joan Allen, up-and-coming young actor Tobey Maguire, and legendary sitcom star Don Knotts, beloved for his roles in shows like *The Andy Griffith Show* and *Three's Company*. Reese was especially excited to have the honor of sharing scenes with Don. "You know what's great about Don [Knotts]? He's one of the most inherently funny men I've ever met," Reese told *Entertainment Tonight*. "He's so funny in this movie. When he had a scene, we would stand, like, a set away and watch, and we were just cracking up. He would just sit funny. And stand funny. He was just so funny in everything he did." And the chance to work with Joan Allen, too, was a thrill for Reese. "She's an inspiration for every young actress," Reese told *Mr. Showbiz*. "She has that calm and reserve about herself and makes you think she appreciates the normal things of every day. Then she transforms into this character that is so different."

Pleasantville was about twins David (Tobey) and Jennifer (Reese), who lead drastically different social lives at their high school. Jennifer is popular, and all the guys in school fawn over her, while David has few friends and cannot talk to the girl he has a crush on. He spends most of his spare time on the couch, watching television, while Jennifer is always out on a date as she is definitely one of the most sexually promiscuous girls in school. For a few months before shooting began, Reese and Tobey hung out together so they could really capture a siblinglike vibe between them. "It was really great because we got to hang out together about three months before filming started. And by the time we started shooting we had the bickering down pat and we knew exactly how irritated to be with each other," Reese told *Entertainment Tonight*. "But it was great, as the movie went on. I felt like we built that dynamic and became more like brother and sister."

When Jennifer and David are left home alone while their single mother goes on vacation with her boyfriend, the twins have a huge fight over what to watch on TV. Jennifer wants to watch a concert with her boyfriend-of-the-week, and David wants to watch a trivia contest about his favorite black and white fifties sitcom, *Pleasantville*. They end up breaking the remote during their fight. Then a mysterious TV repairman (Don Knotts) shows up and gives them a new remote, and when he leaves, they are both transported into the TV and find themselves living in Pleasantville as the characters Bud and Mary Sue Parker. Reese found it very interesting to be transported into that life, which she could not relate to at all. "You hear people talk about how wonderful the fifties were because everything was so simple and pure. Even if that was true—and I don't believe it for a moment—I could have never lived back then. Those poodle skirts, bullet bras, and pageboy hairstyles were the most hideous fashions imaginable," Reese told the *Calgary Sun*. "I thank heaven I can live in a world where I can be as socially free as I want to be. There were so many restrictions for women in the 1950s. Women today are defined by sexuality. That empowers us, but it also places too much emphasis on looks."

The movie starts to take an interesting twist when Jennifer and David's values from the nineties start to infiltrate the innocence of the sexually repressed fifties. When Mary Sue goes on a date with the captain of the basketball team, he has no idea what sex is as they make out in the backseat of his car—until Mary Sue shows him. David, on the other hand, works at the local soda fountain and finds out his boss is miserable with his humdrum life and would rather be an artist, so he gives him an art book. Before long, people in Pleasantville start exploring their sexuality, pursuing their true passions, and leaving the ideals of the fifties behind. Of course, this outrages some—especially when those people who have experienced bursts of passion begin to become colorized. Reese loved the transition her character makes from a girl who only knows how to use her sexuality to get ahead to one who discovers she has a brain, too, and can use it. "The thing that is so ironic about my character is that even though she has the sexual freedom in the '90s, she doesn't find the intellectual freedom until she gets back to the fifties," Reese told *Star Talk*. "Until she starts realizing that things she has to say affect people and educate people. People want to know about sex, well, she has all the answers! You know, it's very empowering. I think through that experience she finds her identity and sort of eventually turns to color."

Making the movie was a professionally rewarding experience for Reese because she really bonded with the cast and crew—it seemed that everyone had mutual respect for each other. "There is no one in this generation who has her chops," Ross told *Vanity Fair*. "Reese is incredibly funny, can hold the center of a comedy, and is unbelievably real at the same time. She will probably win three Oscars. That is honestly the kind of career she can have."

Tobey, too, was in awe of having Reese as his on-screen sibling and costar. "She's got no attitude, which is, you know, rare. She's just a really good actress and she's really funny," Tobey told *Vanity Fair*. "Reese is one of those people that, whenever I bump into her, it just brightens my day. It's not about her vanity. She's here to stay. Slow and steady wins the race."

When Reese had a chance to watch the film, it was a moving

experience for her for several reasons. The first was that it made her appreciative of the life she'd chosen for herself and the era she was lucky enough to be making these decisions in. "The thing that really occurred to me after watching this film is that I am so lucky to have grown up in the time like this when we have the kind of social freedoms that we do. We're not expected to conform in any way," Reese told *Star Talk*. "I think it's so wonderful that teenagers nowadays can express themselves in so many ways, whether they be good or bad. At least they have that kind of freedom of expression and freedom of choice and having dreams and having goals. That's something that is really nice." The other thing that made watching this film different from others she had made was the transition from color to black and white and then back to color. "I thought it was great seeing it for the first time because I think visually—it's something you could never imagine while you're making the movie," Reese told *Entertainment Tonight*. "Actually seeing the black and white and the slow evolution into color was really so striking and dramatic. It was really great to see it. [Seeing ourselves in black and white] was cool, we had a great cinematographer who shot it." And Maguire enjoyed seeing the black-and-white footage for other reasons than the cinematography. "I didn't think I looked too bad, but I thought Reese looked very good in black and white," he told *Entertainment Tonight*.

Pleasantville was critically acclaimed and turned out to be a chance for Reese to really prove herself as a serious—yet comedic—actress. It didn't exactly make her a household name, but it gave her the credibility and respect she needed to eventually book those roles that would make her a star. The reviews were glowing, which was great news for the entire cast, who had bonded and grown as actors during the filming of this special movie. Reese learned a lot about herself and the career she wanted after wrapping *Pleasantville*. "I think it's hard in this business to be or discover the kind of actor that you want to be. I've had my moments in my career where I go, 'I can't believe I made any of those movies before,'" Reese told *Entertainment Tonight*. "Now I know what I am here for and what I really want to do with my career. But, like what happened to my character in *Pleasantville*—it's hard, and I think that there are defining moments where you find yourself in everybody's life." If anything, this role made Reese finally feel secure in having left Stanford and moved to Hollywood. She knew she had made the right decision and was on the right path.

6

The Ballad of Reese and Ryan

Reese may not have been at the forefront of the party scene, but she had her fun and even found herself linked with a few of Hollywood's most sought-after and eligible bachelors. In the early '90s, Chris O'Donnell was one of the hottest young actors around, with a string of hit movies like *School Ties*, *Scent of a Woman*, and *Batman Forever*. Reese would only coyly admit that she had briefly dated O'Donnell, but the two were seen together enough that it was obvious they were more than just friends. When Reese was filming her first real mainstream hit, *Fear*, she was rumored to be dating her costar, Calvin Klein underwear model Mark Wahlberg. It was a short-lived romance—really nothing more than a fling—but it piqued the public's curiosity about Reese as her career started to pick up a little more steam. But, while these brief romances were fun, they weren't full-fledged relationships. Being in love was something Reese had yet to experience . . . until the night of her twenty-first birthday party, at a hot spot called Opium Den in Hollywood.

At the time that Reese was about to turn twenty-one, her career was the main focal point of her life. She was enjoying moderate success and enormous critical acclaim, but she had yet to break through with a blockbuster movie that would put her on the map as a viable and bankable star in Hollywood. To get to that next level, she had to put every ounce of her heart, soul, and time into her career. But in 1997, Reese took a break from being so focused and serious and threw herself a bash to celebrate her birthday. Over three hundred guests—including her dad and brother, who flew in for the festivities from Nashville—showed up to wish her well and toast her with Midori sours, Reese's favorite drink, which she gulped down with gusto that night. As with most Hollywood parties, the host rarely knows more than a handful of the guests personally, and such was the case with Reese that night, though she hardly cared—or noticed. One of those random faceless and nameless guests in attendance was one of the hottest young actors in Hollywood, a twenty-four-year-old guy by the name of Ryan Phillippe. The tall, handsome, and brooding actor was best known for portraying Billy Douglas on *One Life to Live*, the first openly gay character ever on daytime television, and for his starring roles in movies such as *White Squall*. These roles had not only made him a star but also quite the heartthrob among admiring young girls around the country.

Ryan never admitted whether or not he showed up at Reese's party with the intention of introducing himself to her—the way he tells it is that he tagged along with some mutual friends for the "free beer." But what happened when Ryan showed up at the party is a legendary entry in the encyclopedia of great Hollywood romances. Through the mass of people, Ryan made his way over to Reese so he could meet the woman of honor. The pair was formally introduced and a quite inebriated Reese took one look at Ryan's angelic face, ringlets of perfect blond hair, and rock-hard physique, and couldn't help but blurt out, "I think you're my [birthday] present!" Ryan was unfazed, finding her brutal (albeit alcohol-fueled) honesty adorable and irresistible.

For the next hour, Reese and Ryan were engrossed in an intense and mesmerizing conversation. He even insisted on meeting Reese's father and brother. They both couldn't help but be amazed by the connection that they immediately shared. They could have—and would have—kept talking if Ryan hadn't had to cut the evening short. He had to be up at 5 AM the next morning to catch a flight to North Carolina to start filming the horror flick *I Know What You Did Last Summer*. Odds were that their conversation that night would have been their last. This was Hollywood, after all, and Ryan was an eligible bachelor, sought after by thousands of women—famous and not so famous. Plus, he was leaving town the next day for more than three months. And honestly, Reese had met so many people that night at her party (while she was drunk, to boot) that perhaps she wouldn't even remember him the next day. But you can't stop destiny—especially when true love is involved—and there was no way that either of them could forget what had transpired. "I really believe in some sort of controlling fate," Reese told *Allure*. "We immediately hit it off."

For the next two months, Reese and Ryan kept in touch the old-fashioned way with romantic love letters (no e-mail for them) and engaged in elaborate, intense, and revealing phone calls. They also sent each other packages with personal presents such as books they loved so much they wanted the other to read. Reese sent Ryan her beloved book *The End of the Affair* by Graham Greene. "It was wonderful, getting to know who we really were in this sort of pure, antiquated way," Reese recalls. "The letters were not just your typical, 'Hello, how are you, I hope that you're doing well.'" They were sincere, old-fashioned love letters that any girl would melt over. "I would make the letters

sound very Edith Wharton. Kind of like, 'My love—how are you doing?'
We'd never even kissed. The attraction was all mental—we were interested in each other in the most genuine way," Ryan told *TV Guide's Ultimate Cable*. Their late-night phone calls were just as deep and just as
romantic as their letters. "We would have conversations on the phone,
and we hadn't even had our first date. We would cover every subject
imaginable. She would challenge me and I would challenge her. What
struck me most about her was her mind, although she was so adorable
and sexy. I was struck by her individuality—a self-possessed woman
with her own ideas about things," Ryan told *Vanity Fair*.

Reese was amazed by how well getting to know each other more
through correspondence and talking on the telephone than any sort of
physical attraction was working out. "It's so romantic," she gushed to
her friends every time another letter arrived from Ryan. Reese was
wary from past experience, but there was something about Ryan from
the second they started talking that she knew was different. "Before
Ryan, I had a few uncomfortable situations, and they led me to
wanting a relationship that was about somebody respecting my space
and my wishes. Always keep in mind your safety and well-being. The
important thing is that he respects you," Reese told *CosmoGIRL!* "If a
guy tells you he doesn't like your friends or your family, or he says,
'Go change your clothes. I don't like what you're wearing,' you
know that's not *right*. It's your life! You know how you deserve to be
treated, and there should be *no exceptions*."

From their incessant letters and phone calls, both Reese and Ryan
knew exactly what it was about the other that was drawing them in.
"Ryan seemed so sincere and so not into himself," Reese told the *Calgary Sun*. "Too many young actors are so obsessed with themselves, it
makes a relationship near impossible." Ryan was attracted to the type

A side of Reese's personality. "She is incredibly strong and fiercely independent," he told the *Calgary Sun*. "I find that very sexy in a woman."

For two months, Reese and Ryan built their relationship on those intimate letters and phone calls. Then Ryan decided it was time to see if their bliss would hold up in person and invited Reese to come visit him in North Carolina. Reese was in L.A. filming *Pleasantville*. When she found herself with three days off from work to take the trip, she was overcome with cold feet. She wanted to go more than anything, but there was something holding her back—her nerves were getting the best of her, and she couldn't understand why. All this time she had wanted nothing more than to be with Ryan in the flesh. Ryan desperately wanted to see her, too. He knew it was intimidating for a girl to fly across the country to visit a boy she had only met in person once, so he made sure he broached the subject as any gentleman would. He didn't want to put any pressure on Reese or give her the wrong idea about what his intentions for the trip were. He even reminded her that the house he was living in in North Carolina was complete with three bedrooms. "I wasn't going to assume anything," Ryan recalls of their reunion.

Being that Reese had grown up with such a rigorous southern background, Ryan was a perfect match for her. While he wasn't southern himself, he had grown up in New Castle, Delaware, with a close-knit family similar to Reese's own family. And Ryan's parents were excellent role models—just like Reese's—as they were still together and very much in love. His dad was a chemist, and his mother ran a day care center out of their home. Ryan was also the lone boy among three sisters, so he knew the opposite sex from the inside out. "I was dragged to everything, even bridal showers," he says. "It gave me so much understanding. Women tend to be more honest and straight-forward. With guys, it's always about posturing."

Reese confided in her *Pleasantville* costar Tobey Maguire. "I told Tobey, 'I don't know what to do, Ryan wants me to come out there; I'm so conflicted.' And Tobey was like, 'You know what, Reese? I've heard you talk about him. I can tell how crazy you are about him. And you should totally do it. Because if some girl did that for me, it would simply make my lifetime,'" Reese told *Allure*.

So, Reese listened to Maguire and realized he was right. She soon found herself on autopilot, making the necessary arrangements to get on the first flight to North Carolina. It didn't even faze her when she couldn't find a direct flight—all that mattered was seeing in the flesh her pen pal from the past two months, who spoke directly to her soul. As Reese walked off the plane, she found herself beyond exhausted from her travels and layovers and inside a tiny airport that seemed like it was in the middle of nowhere. But it didn't matter. Reese looked up and saw Ryan waiting for her. What should have been one of the most romantic moments of her entire life turned into a moment of utter panic. Reese looked into Ryan's eyes and couldn't help but freak out all over again. "I was like, 'Oh, my God, I don't even know you,'" Reese recalls of that pivotal moment. "I suddenly thought, 'What am I doing here? I came all this way and I don't even know him. He could be a serial killer!'" Ryan watched as the color drained out of Reese's face and fear darted from her eyes. "The first thing she said to me when she got off the plane was 'I shouldn't have come alone. I have to go call my mother.'" Reese wasn't kidding. She excused herself to go and find the nearest phone to call her mother in Nashville for a dose of reality. "I was, like, 'Mother, am I just crazy?' And she was, like, 'No, Reese. You really like him.'" All it took was the voice of reason from her mom on the other end to bring Reese back to reality—and remind her of the reason why she had made this journey—to follow her heart. With just letters and phone calls as their main courtship, she had found herself falling in love with Ryan whether she wanted to admit it or not. Now that they were able to take that connection to the next level—in person—Reese took a deep breath, let her inhibitions go, and decided to let fate take over for the next three days of her trip. Those days passed by in a blur as Reese and Ryan deepened their bond in person and both realized that this was the real deal. When Reese boarded the plane to head back home to L.A., she was giddy as a schoolgirl, because she was no longer fighting what she knew to be true. Reese was truly, madly, deeply in love with Ryan. Ryan, too, knew without a doubt that he had officially fallen in love with her that weekend.

When Ryan returned to L.A. just a few months later, the two continued their relationship as if they had never been apart and as if they had been together forever. Reese felt so comfortable with Ryan so early on that she told her friends it was as if they were already an old married couple. "We were so comfortable with each other. I really believe I was meant to find this person in my life, and he was meant to find me, and we were meant to be together," Reese told *Allure*. "I feel very corny talking about it, but I am just overwhelmed with a sense that it chose us; we didn't choose it."

7

Cruel Intentions *Turn into Pleasant Surprise*

A few months into their relationship, Ryan signed on to star with his *I Know What You Did Last Summer* costar Sarah Michelle Gellar in a take on *Dangerous Liaisons* set in the world of bored, rich, upper-crust teenagers in New York City. The movie was called *Cruel Intentions*. Ryan signed on to play the scheming, arrogant Sebastian, stepbrother to the evil, manipulative Katherine, played by Gellar. The stepsiblings make a bet that Sebastian, a Lothario who has bedded almost every young girl in Manhattan, can deflower the pure and innocent Annette Hargrove after they read an article she writes in *Seventeen* about why she is saving herself for marriage. She is also the daughter of the new headmaster at their ritzy private school. Things take a twist when Sebastian finds himself falling in love with Annette instead of just toying with her affections. Annette, who starts out seeing right through Sebastian's act, begins to develop real feelings for him, too. She can't control herself, breaks her vow, and makes love with Sebastian. Things of course get complicated when Katherine blackmails Sebastian into breaking up with her.

Ryan could not imagine anyone other than Reese playing the role of Annette. Roger Kumble, the director of the film, could not have agreed with Ryan more, and the two were in cahoots to convince Reese that this was a role she could not afford to pass on. Reese, however, had just done three movies back to back and was looking forward to taking a nice, long break before choosing her next project. When Ryan and Kumble first brought up the movie to Reese, she begged them not to pressure her and tried to make them understand that she just couldn't do it—she was too exhausted.

Ryan and Kumble refused to give up without a fight, because they knew the movie would not have the same impact without Reese on board. So they took Reese out to dinner, made sure there was plenty of wine flowing, and, when they thought she was drunk enough, they asked her again. "They said, 'Please do this,' and I thought, 'Why not? It will be great to work with Ryan,'" Reese recalls.

While Reese remembers it being an easy sell, Kumble remembers selling Reese on the part being a bit trickier. "I got down on my knees at Le Petit Bistro and begged her, 'Please! *Please!* Reese, you have to do this!'" he says. Between Kumble's pleading and her boyfriend's unwavering insistence that she sign on, Reese couldn't help but say yes. There was, however, a catch. The character of Annette had to be rewritten per Reese's approval. "In the original script she was more like the *Dangerous Liaisons* character, timid and shy, and it didn't make sense to me," Reese explains. "She'd be devoured by these predatory people! I made her an intellectual, a woman wedded to her principles, and it made her seem more attainable in a very different way."

Now that the script was to Reese's liking and the ink on her contract was dry, it was Ryan who started to have some pangs of doubt and concern about Reese as his costar. "What if this movie stinks? And I pulled my girlfriend into this and it's going to be a mess?" Ryan kept thinking to himself. "If this thing is a piece of shit, it's going to be all my fault." The other thing Ryan worried about was that having Reese on set meant she was going to be keeping him on his toes and watching his performance with a critical eye. "She was going to know if I was half-assing it," he says.

Ryan had little to worry about. One night, Reese stayed late on the set and watched some of Ryan's scenes from the screening room. She couldn't believe it. Reese was so moved by Ryan's performance that it brought tears to her eyes. She called him, crying, to let him know. "It was the best telephone call I've ever had," Ryan recalls.

Tears on the set of *Cruel Intentions* were actually a common occurrence for Reese and Ryan. Their characters go through many emotional highs and lows together, including an intense and unsettling breakup scene that taxed not only their acting abilities but also their relationship. "I actually threw up the day we started filming that scene because I got so worked up," says Ryan. "I mean, looking at Reese and saying those things . . . she was amazing, so strong as an actress and a person. I think I'm a little softer than she is, so it was harder for me." As tough as Reese was, the vicious words they were not only saying to each other but also had to make believable were almost too much for Reese to bear. She recalls: "Ryan was off camera giving me my lines and he started to ad-lib, saying things like: 'I've never loved you! You're not attractive!' Terrible things. I got so upset. I just hauled off and socked him in the face, and everybody was like, 'Gasp! Can you believe she just did that?' And I'm screaming my lines and I just yelled *'Get out'* and he just ran off and threw up in a stairwell and I'm sobbing and the director came in and said, 'Oh, God, that was so great! Can you do it again?'"

At the end of the day, Ryan had a bright red cheek and the two had to go home together and resume their "real-life" relationship without letting the work they had just done—even though it was acting—

affect them. "Of course, we knew it was only acting," says Reese. "But having to say all those nasty things to each other for a whole day was very difficult and emotionally draining." If anything, making the movie was beneficial to them on many levels. For one thing, Reese thought it made their relationship stronger—and therefore the film better. "Our personal relationship added something to the film since our characters have innate chemistry with each other," Reese explained. "We try to maintain a sense of privacy. But we gave of ourselves, and I think our relationship really shows in a couple of places."

8

And Baby Makes Three . . .

In the months after *Cruel Intentions* wrapped, Reese and Ryan's relationship continued to deepen. They were living together and enjoying a very low-key life when they weren't on movie sets or gracing red carpets. *Cruel Intentions* was scheduled to hit theaters on March 5, 1999. In the meantime, Reese and Ryan went back to work on various movies until it was time to promote the film—as well as start planning for their future together. In December 1998, Ryan whisked Reese away to the Planters Inn in Charleston, South Carolina, for a romantic getaway. Over breakfast in bed—Reese's favorite of waffles with strawberries and cream—Ryan got into bed with Reese and proposed. Reese excitedly said yes, and the two couldn't wait to start planning the rest of their lives together. Because they were young and in the public eye, they decided to let the engagement be something just the two of them would share for a while—only telling people they trusted and felt close to, like their families. "I haven't had a lot of what most people would consider serious relationships, and this is definitely the first time I've been in love," Ryan told the *Calgary Sun* of his relationship with Reese.

To Reese, marriage was an important step, as she took the joining of their lives and honoring of their family values seriously. "My family is very important to me, and I have a very close family, including my husband's side," Reese told *Flare*. "Ryan is a big grounding influence on my life. Also, my parents instilled in me a strong work ethic and very strong family values. The most important thing no matter what is building a strong family who will care for you." Speculation and rumors started floating in the press that perhaps the couple was engaged. Rather than answer flat out, Reese told the *Calgary Sun*, "I certainly haven't thought of getting engaged before, and the whole idea of marriage is very new to me. Ryan and I haven't set a date, but it's definitely in our future." With the wedding a future event in their lives, Reese and Ryan got ready to start their promotional duties for *Cruel Intentions* and even decided that they would move from L.A. to New York City—a place they both fell in love with while making *Cruel Intentions*. Then something happened that threw all their plans off course. They were no longer going to be able to be quite so coy about their wedding plans when Reese discovered that she was expecting a baby.

For many young actors, news of a baby could be devastating, as it could be a career ender. Unfortunately, not all women—famous or not—have a guy to love and support them and see the baby as a blessing instead of a disaster. For Reese, she had her soul mate Ryan by her side, and while getting married and having children were in their plans, it wasn't something they were expecting this early on. "I never thought I would have a family so young, but you can't plan everything," Reese told *What*. "I'm sort of a roll-with-the-punches sort of person anyway. My life takes a lot of planning, a lot of organizing. But I feel very lucky. I was surprised [I was pregnant] but pleasantly so. I was a bit scared at first. Now I've really come into my own and have a better perspective."

Reese and Ryan took the news of their baby as a blessing. And Reese believed that she could be a wife, mother, and actress without missing a beat. "I certainly think that with these things, no matter how much planning goes into them, they choose you; you don't choose them."

"The pregnancy was not planned, but it was a wonderful surprise," Reese told *Allure*. "The battles that we face in this business aren't financial, but they are moral. And I certainly think that the longer you can keep your values, and your family values, and your morality intact, and keep your head on your shoulders about what is important at the end of the day, you can get the most out of this business and really emerge with something wonderful."

Reese did have some apprehension about her pregnancy—especially since she was far away from her mother, with whom she was so close. "I was scared to death and I didn't know what I was doing. I was in L.A. and my mother was in Tennessee, and I don't have any sisters, so I felt so alone," Reese told *Good Housekeeping*. "I went to a prenatal yoga class because it was the only place I'd heard about where there were other pregnant women. Finally, one of these women there said, 'Would you like to come over after you have your baby and have a play date with me and my baby?' And I just screamed, 'Yes! What time? Can I bring some muffins?' It was a great thing to have that support." She also started to feel her hormones kick into overdrive. "The slightest thing can just make me sob and weep for hours. Like yesterday I saw on television a Humane Society commercial and I cried for three hours. They were talking about these poor animals and it made me just want to go down there," Reese told Conan O'Brien. "And you know people beat their dogs to death and all this stuff and I was just crying for three hours. It was awful." But when all was said and done, despite having the normal fears and concerns that every expectant couple experiences, Reese and Ryan were both on cloud nine. "We're ecstatic. I thought that my best friend from high school was going to be so shocked, but she said wonderful things to me. She said, 'I think you of all people are ready for this,'" Reese said. "That made me feel so much better about things. The fact that people really believe in you is wonderful." The people Reese wasn't so sure would understand were her fiercely traditional southern relatives. "I said, 'Grandma—I have good news! I'm getting married!' And she's like 'Great!' and then I said, 'Oh, I have more good news—I'm having a baby!'" Reese told *Newsweek* of the experience of telling her family. "I love my grandma. It was a little hard for her at first and that breaks my heart."

As Reese experienced morning sickness and starting developing a slight bump in her midsection, their secret was about to be revealed to the rest of the world whether they were ready or not. So in March, as Reese and Ryan joined the rest of their *Cruel Intentions* cast mates on the red carpet of the movie's premiere, they told the world that they were more in love than ever, engaged to be married, and expecting their first child together. A whirlwind of press and attention followed. Reese and Ryan were already an adored Hollywood couple among their fans. Their love for each other seemed to radiate in such a way that people rooted for them and wanted them to be happy and together forever. They weren't ostentatious or grandiose about their relationship in public, because they didn't have to do anything to let the world know how devoted they were to each other except hold hands and look at each other adoringly. Now that the golden couple was expecting a baby, it just made their fairy-tale image complete. "It is the most incredible thing that has happened to me, and I feel so lucky to have found the person I want to be with," Ryan told *Allure*.

At this same time, *Cruel Intentions* was released to mixed reviews but became a smash hit among teens and twentysomethings and went on to gross $40 million worldwide. Reese and Ryan entered a new level of fame because of the popularity of the film. They went from recognizable celebrities with their own fan bases to bona fide stars who could sell magazines if their faces were on the covers and open movies with big grosses if their names were on the marquee. The types of scripts and roles that Reese and Ryan both started to get offered were more high-profile than anything they had been offered before.

On June 5, 1999, Reese and Ryan went back to the city where they had gotten engaged—Charleston, South Carolina—and had a small wedding ceremony on a plantation with both their families by their sides. Reese was seven months pregnant but wore a virginal white lace wedding dress because that was what she always envisioned she would be wearing as she walked down the aisle. Ryan wore traditional attire for the South—tan linen. The sweet, small, and simple ceremony featured a gospel choir singing "At Last" as they officially joined together as husband and wife.

Marriage and family were integral parts of both Reese and Ryan's upbringings, so they were committed to making things work despite so many major life experiences hitting them at such a young age. At their wedding, Ryan was twenty-five and Reese was twenty-three. "Ryan and I both grew up with parents who have been married over thirty years and I think it has taught us both a lesson about commitment and how important it is not to just throw up your hands about this or that," Reese told *Good Housekeeping*. "I'm very lucky. I have a very wonderful, giving husband, a really loving person. He really knows who he is and where he belongs and what he wants out of life."

Being pregnant was a special time for Reese, who really enjoyed it. "I didn't have morning sickness. And I've been feeling so wonderful and healthy and happy," she told AOL. "I've had a few weird cravings like root beer, grape juice, and seafood. I never even liked seafood before. But now I'm ravenous for it. I guess you crave stuff your body needs." In fact, Reese ate so many grapes and drank so much grape juice that she would joke with her friends that she wouldn't be surprised if she gave birth to a grape! To get through the emotional roller coaster of pregnancy, Reese had daily phone conversations with her mother; this helped ease her fears and calm her growing nerves as it grew closer to her due date. Reese and Ryan also decided that they wanted to find out the sex of the baby before it was born. Ever the type A, Reese was positive she was carrying a boy, but the ultrasound revealed otherwise. "I was surprised when the ultrasound revealed that I was having a girl, I was convinced I was having a boy," Reese told *InStyle*. "And I was completely confounded by the fact that I wasn't in control of the situation—that I was being introduced to a different individual coming into my life."

Reese and Ryan were excited, expectant parents and, despite the fact that both their careers were on an upswing after the success of *Cruel Intentions*, their priority remained their unborn baby. "I'm very excited about the baby. I realize no movie can ever be as important as the process and journey we're going through now," Reese told the *Los Angeles Daily News* while she was pregnant in 1999. "I think that it's very easy to take time in your life to work on your career, but it's harder to take time to work on the quality of your life. But that's what we plan on doing for the next year." Reese kept a level head about what having a baby might mean for her career and for future choices that she was going to make. "I don't know if my tastes will change after I have the baby. You make decisions on who you are as a person, but I don't know how that's going to affect me," Reese speculated to the *Los Angeles Daily News*. "I'm definitely happy with the way my career has gone, the success. But I even feel glad that I've experienced some failure in my life. That gives you perspective and humility about this business. It's good to realize that you're always just one movie away from not being in vogue anymore."

It was hard, but Reese never let it show if she was having any doubts or fears about being a young mother and, as a result, losing her standing in Hollywood. "I don't know [how the baby is going to affect my career]! We'll just see how it happens. Obviously this isn't the time in my life that I would have chosen to do this, but I feel like life gives you these challenges for a reason," Reese told *ET Online*. "I feel so happy and glad to be in the place that I am. I really feel blessed. This is something I need to face and take control of. I feel really, really good. I've been having a great time and I'm really enjoying myself. I feel so great to be young and have this experience."

After nine months, Reese and Ryan welcomed their first child into the world. Their daughter, Ava Elizabeth Phillippe, was born on September 9, 1999. She was named in honor of Ryan's grandmother. Reese was nervous about holding her newborn daughter, but Ryan's mom had a day care center in their home, so he had grown up with babies and children around all the time. "Reese had never held a baby until our own, whereas I grew up taking care of kids so it was a much more natural transition for me," Ryan said. "What impresses me most is her ability as a mother. She constantly keeps me excited and engaged and I'm always interested to hear what's on her mind." As Reese and Ryan got used to late-night feedings and diaper changing, Reese also got a clearer picture of what motherhood meant to her and what kind of mother and role model she wanted to be for Ava. "A new child puts your life into perspective. You realize the most important thing is being a good person, so that your daughter or your child grows up having the right kind of values. So I've put a lot of focus on being the best person I can be for my child, and that's changed me quite a bit," Reese explained to AOL. "You wake up one day and say, 'This is who I have been and this is who I want to be to this child, how I want her to see me as a woman, as a mother and a wife,'" Reese told *W*. "I used to be so much more competitive, caught up in the why so-and-so got that job and I didn't. I had to let it go because it's all so arbitrary and never very personal. You have to be cool with what's yours, and I've got mine, and what's mine is good." Motherhood, however, was a tough adjustment for Reese, as it was nothing like what she had imagined it would be like while she was pregnant. The first six weeks were the hardest. "[Motherhood] is a lot of work. Yeah, they don't tell you. They don't warn you. It was just a lot of work," Reese told Jay Leno. "Yeah, I would stand over the crib sometimes and just go, 'Please sleep. Please sleep. Please go to sleep!'" And like many new mothers, Reese started to doubt whether she was cut out for taking care of another human being, and that took a toll on her relationship with Ryan. "I never held a newborn before Ava. So when she was thrust upon me, it was like, 'What do I do?' It was hard," Reese told *Cosmopolitan*. "I was trying to understand my new position as a woman and what it all meant. I went through a long period when I was really depressed and I couldn't figure out why. When you're living your life, sometimes it's hard to see how wonderful it is. I finally realized I had this wonderful guy and child, and I wasn't going to throw it away by being miserable." As time went by and Reese adjusted to not getting as much sleep as she used to, she finally settled into motherhood and started to enjoy parenthood with Ryan. "We love being parents. We love the simple joy of watching Ava in the morning. It's really soothing," Reese told *InStyle*. "What we do is so hectic and exhausting. It's so nice to have that comfort and stability at home." And when Reese was feeling unsure of things, her mom was a phone call away for her, just as she had been during her pregnancy. "My mom had a lot of advice for me. Number one being 'Don't drop the baby. Especially on her head.' So that was good," Reese told Jay Leno. "And I call her whenever I have problems and I'm all panicked. And you know, she taught me how to change diapers and everything. So it was very helpful."

9

Meet Tracy Flick

After a few months, Reese and Ryan had adjusted to parenthood and started to feel comfortable with this change in their lives. It was time for both of them to start talking about how they were going to have careers, too. The first rule they came up with was that neither of them could be gone longer than two weeks on a movie set, and only one of them could be away at a time. "When Ryan is working, I'm at home. When I'm working, he's there. Of course, we have babysitters, but Ava is very much our center of interest," Reese told the *Tennessean*. "Everybody keeps reminding us of the frailty of Hollywood marriages, but I don't pay much attention. We have strong family ties, both of our parents are still together." They were adamant that family had to come first, over their movie careers. "No movie is so important that it would be worth sacrificing our family life," Ryan told *Vanity Fair*. And while they both were entertaining movie offers and trying to decide on what their next respective career moves should be, Ryan was OK with Reese's career taking precedence. "Once you've made the decision to start a family, the importance of work seems to go down a bit! I mean, I love what I do, but I don't think there'll ever be one movie where I feel like I have to do it. Actually I kind of like Reese to do all the acting!" Ryan told *TV Hits Yearbook*. "Someday I'd like to get into some producing, where the focus isn't so much on me—that would be cool. We're working on a system where if Reese works, then I don't! I mean, I'll go on location with her and sit with the baby and vice versa. I think it's even more difficult for the women to take a career risk like this, and I admire her for it. She has enough confidence in her abilities to know she'll be able to work as an actress and she's been so focused on having the baby, too. It is difficult, though, especially as this is the best our careers have ever been."

As they both tried to figure out what was next, careerwise, Reese and Ryan settled into a very quiet lifestyle that was very un-Hollywood-like. "We both cook and enjoy doing that together," Ryan told *Vanity Fair*. "Reese didn't know how to cook very well when we first met. I remember the first meal she tried to make me was Hamburger Helper. She has come a long way." This time in their lives was probably the most stressful and trying, but Reese and Ryan were closer than ever. "I thank God Ryan and I got married. There are times when you think, 'Are these the right decisions that I'm making?'" Reese told *Vanity Fair*. "Ultimately, I think it has been really helpful to have the person who knows me so well for a husband, who experiences the same kind of frustrations and lives the same lifestyle." The frustrations that Reese and Ryan were facing were one and the same—how could they top the success of *Cruel Intentions* and keep building the momentum in their careers?

Reese, while pregnant with Ava, released a film called *Election* in May 1999. While *Cruel Intentions* built her young fan base and made her more of a household name, *Election* told the industry that she was more than just another Hollywood blonde—this southern belle could act! Ryan, however, would not release another movie until September

2000 with the disappointing *The Way of the Gun* with Benicio Del Toro. At the time, it seemed he was perfectly happy to let his wife take the spotlight, and it seemed that both of them were more interested in their family than in their careers. Except that *Election*, while a small film, grew to be vital for Reese's career.

The movie is a black comedy that takes a satirical look at high school politics. It is based on a critically acclaimed novel of the same name written by Tom Perrotta. Reese played übersuccessful and driven high school senior Tracy Flick, who starts out running for student body president unopposed. "I describe her as a chronic over-achiever," Reese told *Mr. Showbiz*. "She's a type A personality, very serious and a member of every club so it will go on her college application. You find out, though, that she's actually a lonely kid and has no friends." Matthew Broderick narrates the film and plays history teacher Mr. McAllister, who is rubbed the wrong way by Tracy for several reasons. For one, he knows her "Little Miss Perfect" act is flawed, considering that Tracy had an affair with a former teacher, causing his dismissal. "Matthew Broderick's character describes her as a young Adolf Hitler," says Reese. He just finds everything about Tracy annoying and can't bear Tracy having the satisfaction of running unopposed. To put an end to that, Mr. McAllister convinces the school jock Paul Metzler, played by Chris Klein, to run against her, which in turn leads his lesbian sister, Tammy, to run because Paul is dating her ex-girlfriend. With three contestants vying for the presidency, Tracy Flick does everything to play by the rules and win, while Mr. McAllister does everything he can to sabotage her efforts.

Reese embodied the character of Tracy Flick, with her prim, proper, and irritating speaking voice and soul-piercing facial expressions. The way Reese played Tracy, you could feel her overachieving, perfectionist

ways oozing out of her. The director of the movie was Alexander
Payne, who had done films such as *Citizen Ruth* but would go on to
direct Oscar-nominated films like *About Schmidt* with Jack Nicholson
and *Sideways* with Paul Giamatti. He had seen Reese's first movie, *The
Man in the Moon*, and was absolutely taken with her talent. When he
took on *Election*, she was the only actress he could envision playing the
part of Tracy. "She has such intelligence and humor," Payne told *Allure*.
"Working with her, I kept thinking Holly Hunter—she is an actress who
is equally at home in character roles and in leads and in comedy and
drama. Reese has that kind of range as an actress and a human being."

Reese was unaware that Payne had been following her career, but
when she read the script, she knew that she was destined to play Tracy.
"I walked into Alexander Payne's office and I said, 'You can hire somebody else but you are going to make the wrong decision. You should
hire me because I am this part,'" Reese revealed on the *Charlie Rose
Show*. "I just knew what to do with it and I knew I was going to be great
at it. And I don't know where it came from, but he called me at the
end of the week. I met him on a Monday and on Friday I had the job."

It was ironic for Reese to play a go-getter with such a rigorous way
of doing things, considering that Reese herself had similar qualities—
she was called "Little Miss Type A" by her own parents, after all. But
Reese was nowhere near as meticulous and precise as Tracy—and had
a lot more friends, too. "It's great because this character reminded me
of so many people. One of those horrible people who are so perfect,
you just want to kill them, but you can't because they are so perfect,
and they get you in the end anyway. It's great to be able to bring that to
the screen. You have this character who, for all intents and purposes, is
likable, but you just can't stand her," Reese said. "There was a girl in my
junior high school who was so perfect, always had all the boyfriends,

and I hated her. She was nice but in a backhanded way, so this was kind of my little revenge. I wore my hair similar to how she wore her hair."

But Reese wasn't going to let memories of an archenemy from junior high be the sole basis of her character. She decided to update her ideas of high school by going incognito to a school where they were filming, in Omaha, Nebraska. "It was interesting because I had been three or four years out of high school [when she made *Election*]," Reese told *Girlfriend*. "I think you tend to block out your whole high school experience, most people do, because it is so traumatic." Reese met a girl who was president of the student council and a cheerleader who took her under her wing and showed her around the school. "She was such an inspiration for the character," Reese told the *Los Angeles Daily News*. But by the second day, the students at the school started to catch on and realize who Reese really was. "People were throwing stuff at me in the cafeteria, saying, 'You're Reese Witherspoon! Why don't you just tell us who you are? This is ridiculous!'" Reese recalled to *ET Online*. "At the end of the day I went on the PA and told everybody that I was who they thought I was. But it was really interesting, the trauma of walking into a cafeteria and not knowing where I was going to sit and not knowing who my friends were. Oh, it was just awful!" Reese found it equally helpful to be around kids who had grown up in Omaha, since that was the movie's setting. She ultimately developed Tracy's voice using the accents of the kids she had met. Payne could not have been more pleased with the research Reese did to nail the nuances and distinguishing idiosyncrasies of Tracy. "She's the real McCoy," he told *Premiere*. "She concocted that voice, that walk, and I swear her eyebrows are individually wired. She's really frank."

Coming on to the set of *Election*, Reese was particularly excited because her costar Matthew Broderick was one of her favorite actors.

She counted his film *Ferris Bueller's Day Off* among her favorites. She even admitted that she was more nervous about acting alongside Matthew than she had been with her *Twilight* costar Paul Newman. "I got so excited when they called and told me that Matthew was going to be playing the role of Mr. McAllister. I watched every one of his movies when I was little and I probably had a little crush on him," Reese told *ET Online*. "I just thought he was so funny and it's great to see in this movie that it's sort of the return of Matthew Broderick as the guy that you love to laugh at in the movies." Matthew was just as impressed with Reese, calling her a "small package filled with power" to *Premiere*. The rest of the cast was made up mostly of unknown actors.

Election was Chris Klein's first movie, as he had yet to star in the colossal hit *American Pie*. He landed the role of Paul Metzler when Payne was scouting his high school as a location to shoot the movie. He met Klein in the hall and the rest, as they say, is history. "I really liked the fact that there were sort of so many unknown actors. It made you feel like they really are these people [in the movie] or could be," Reese told *Star Interviews*. "You get more of a sense of reality to it." Reese, however, thought that Tracy was too cartoonish for her to really relate to, or at least compare to her high school self. "Tracy was so bizarre and over the top. She's such a chronic overachiever," Reese told *ET Online*. "I wasn't that motivated in high school. I was doing movies at the same time so I was just trying to make people *not* notice me. But I liked Tracy because she is one of those people who wants it all and is determined to get it all. I think she doesn't understand that life is important, too. But she's certainly very funny and goes about it in a funny way, so she's fun to watch."

As filming for *Election* got under way, Reese became attached to the character of Tracy Flick and stayed in character even when she wasn't filming. "I would come somewhat in character to the set. I would be all perky and high-energy, and I would pester Matthew Broderick like an annoying little sister," Reese told *ET Online*. "We had a great rapport with each other. It was fun."

Though playing the role of Tracy did have its downside. "I smiled so much in the movie I got, like, TMJ at the end of the day," she told Conan O'Brien. "I had such a jaw ache that I thought I would never recover." Reese saw *Election* as one of her greatest acting experiences to date and hoped that the moviegoing public would feel the same way upon its release. "This was definitely an important film and a real labor of love. I had such a good time, and it was a character I got into," Reese told *Mr. Showbiz*. "I describe it as a comedy about the nuances of everyday life and the ennui of everyday life and the reality of that."

Election was by no means a smash success. It was released in a limited number of theaters and didn't have a blockbuster opening weekend, but slowly, word of mouth about the dark comedy spread. And while *Election* garnered Reese the best reviews of her career to date and even earned her a Golden Globe nomination for Best Actress in a Musical or Comedy, the movie actually ended up hurting her career and the way she was seen in Hollywood casting offices.

Reese found that even her fans and people she would encounter in her day-to-day life started to treat her differently—because she embodied the character so well, they thought that the grating and annoying Tracy Flick was what Reese was really like in real life! It was a stretch, but it wasn't a completely wrong assumption. "People were really scared of me and would walk around me because they thought I was Tracy Flick," Reese told *Vanity Fair*. "And *part* of me is like that character. I think there is no way to hide parts of yourself. There is a reason you are attracted to roles."

The film came out just a few months before Reese gave birth to Ava, so she was planning on taking an unofficial maternity leave from Hollywood. The reviews for *Election* were glowing. Leah Rozen from *People* said, "Witherspoon, her face permanently scrunched in determination, gives a wonderfully witty performance as the girl most likely—no matter what it takes—to succeed." So with the critics on her side, Reese never imagined that, when she was ready to start reading scripts and auditioning again, so many doors would end up closing in her face. One problem was that the movie was yet another one in which Reese played a teenager. Even though this was her most mature and original work to date, it followed teen characters in *Fear*, *Pleasantville*, and *Cruel Intentions*. Reese was twenty-three years old when *Election* was released. "I try to not to think of any of my roles as teen stereotypes," Reese told *Mr. Showbiz*. "I look at them as characters and Tracy, for an actress of any age, is irresistible—an obsessive-compulsive type A." Reese was disappointed when many critics—despite the rave reviews—still classified *Election* as another teen movie. "I found that very confusing," Reese told *Daily Express*. "It's actually about a guy going through a midlife crisis and just happens to be set in high school. It's a very mature film, but getting that word out is tough." Reese didn't want to be pigeonholed into doing teenage films but also didn't want to turn down the opportunity to play such well-developed characters as Tracy Flick. "I don't really think about the genre of the film when I'm doing it," she told TNT's *Rough Cut*. "I just loved the script and it's hard when people go, 'You want to do another teenage movie?' And I just say, 'But the character is so great.'"

No matter how Reese justified why she'd agreed to play Tracy Flick, and despite the fact that Tracy earned her rave reviews, accolades, and a permanent place in pop culture history as a memorable brownnoser, it hurt Reese's career where it really mattered. "I couldn't get a job after *Election*. It was a great experience, though, and very well reviewed. It was one of those films that people found out about after it came out. But afterwards I could not get a job. They wouldn't let me audition to be the best friend in some movies. I was despondent. I think because the character I played was so extreme and shrewish—some people thought that is who I was, rather than me going in and creating a part," Reese told *Interview*. "I would audition for things and I'd always be the second choice. Studios never wanted to hire me, and I wasn't losing the parts to big box office actresses, but to ones I guess people felt differently about. I'd get letters from the directors saying, 'I loved your audition, I really wanted to cast you, but the studio won't let me.' I have a stack of them."

10

Don't Call Us, We'll Call You

If Tracy Flick, Reese's character in *Election*, had been faced with the closed doors and unfair discrimination that Reese was dealing with after the release of the movie, she surely wouldn't have taken it lying down. Tracy would have been in casting offices with lists of reasons why they were wrong to blow her off—and a few ass-kissing tactics thrown in for good measure. Reese, however, decided to just lie low. She had played the character of Tracy *too* well, if that was possible, and while critics thought she was brilliant, movie studios thought that if she was playing a character so abrasively, it couldn't be all acting and they didn't want to risk having a real-life Tracy Flick to contend with. The "Little Miss Type A" in Reese should have come out fighting to tell Hollywood how unfair and discriminatory they were being. But with a husband and baby daughter in her life now, her career, while still very important, was no longer the main priority. Reese decided to appreciate being second choice and enjoy flying under the radar so she could spend more time with her family.

Ryan was working steadily and hoping that the slate of movies he was filming would be well received to give his career the kind of boost it had gotten when *Cruel Intentions* came out. Respect in Hollywood was not an issue for Ryan; one of the movies he was working on was an adaptation of *Gosford Park* helmed by legendary director Robert Altman— most actors could only dream of being cast in one of his movies.

Reese found herself taking smaller parts in movies, such as the Adam Sandler comedy *Little Nicky*, where she had only a cameo as an angel waiting at the gates of heaven. Then she had a small, albeit memorable, role in the disturbing adaptation of the Bret Easton Ellis novel *American Psycho*. When it was announced that *American Psycho* was being turned into a movie, there was great debate over how such a graphic and violent story could be made into a film that would be allowed into theaters. The book was about an arrogant and spoiled yuppie named Patrick Bateman living a life of privilege and prestige by day, and going on unthinkable and deranged killing sprees by night. The gruesome and vivid details of the killings in the book made people in the film industry nervous. Christian Bale, who was best known for his role in *Empire of the Sun* when he was just a child, and who had gone on to star in movies like *Little Women*, *Newsies*, and *Swing Kids*, was signed on to play the role of Patrick.

Reese was up for the role of Patrick's spoiled fiancé Evelyn, and she also had her concerns about signing on for such a controversial film. She met with the film's director, Mary Harron, who had previously directed the well received *I Shot Andy Warhol*—which dealt with equally sensitive material. *I Shot Andy Warhol* was based on the true story of Valerie Solanas, who shot (but did not kill) the famous pop artist as a statement against the arrogant domination of male power figures. Harron was praised for not glorifying Valerie in the film, but painting a fair and unbiased picture of why she took her anger out on Andy Warhol specifically.

Harron's vision for *American Psycho* the movie was very different from *American Psycho* the novel. The novel was notorious for being misogynistic and gruesome, but Mary wanted to make the film satirical—and even humorous—to make fun of Patrick's materialism and dig into the deeper meanings of his urges to kill. Reese was thrilled that they were on the same page. Even though her role was small, Reese was not going to let that affect her performance or preparation for getting into character. "Obviously I had to be sure about this role. I read the book and had a long discussion with director Mary Harron, and we had a sort of similar view about the film," Reese explained to the *Toronto Sun*. "To me, the move is a dark satire of a male response to the sexual liberation of women in the early '80s. That women didn't need men was a new thing for these young men who were doing everything possible to be impressive and wearing these designer shoes and having these wonderful apartments and spending this money and women just didn't give a shit."

Reese was excited that the movie was going to take on a fresh perspective, and that the novel would be toned down and rendered less violent. "I don't think we could have had all that rampant killing and still maintain a story," she said. "There's only really one violent sequence in the whole movie. It's about a two- to three-minute sequence. So, it really is different [from the book]. It takes different aspects of the book rather than chopping up and cooking people and eating them." Reese was also excited to have the chance to work alongside Christian Bale, as he was an actor she respected and admired. "I am so happy Christian got to make the film. He is the main reason I did it," Reese told *Daily Express*. "I've pretty much seen all his work since *Empire of the Sun* and I was so excited to work with him. He's really a wonderful actor who makes very smart decisions and doesn't ever compromise his integrity." The movie opened to mixed reviews, though the focus was not on Reese, as her part was too small to garner any real attention. Most reviews didn't even mention her character or performance. So while it was great for her résumé that she had acted in a movie out of her comfort zone like *American Psycho*, because she wasn't the star and didn't have a memorable role, it didn't help undo any of the damage from *Election*.

To try and get back in front of the eyes of mainstream America, in 2000 Reese booked a guest-starring role on the biggest and most watched American sitcom—*Friends*. The show had launched the careers of Jennifer Aniston, Courteney Cox, Lisa Kudrow, Matthew Perry, Matt LeBlanc, and David Schwimmer; they played a group of Manhattanites trying to figure out life, love, and their careers.

When Reese came on board, the show was in its sixth season and was famous for its A-list guest stars. Reese was following in the footsteps of Brooke Shields, Tom Selleck, and Ben Stiller, all of whom had guested before her. For two episodes she was going to play Jill Greene, the younger sister of Rachel (played by Jennifer Aniston). Jill arrives at Rachel's doorstep after she has a fight with their father and decides she needs to be independent. Though, vapid and spoiled as Jill is, her idea of independence includes a lot of shopping and being pampered instead of job searching and cutting up the credit cards in their father's name (as Rachel suggests). Then things take an interesting twist when Rachel fears that Jill is falling for her ex-boyfriend, Ross (played by David Schwimmer); of course, she is vehemently opposed to them dating. In the end, Jill decides that Ross isn't the one for her, makes up with her father, and goes back home to Long Island.

Reese was thrilled to have the opportunity to be on *Friends* because she had been addicted to watching the show while she was pregnant with Ava. The experience of performing in front of a live audience was also exhilarating—as well as terrifying—to Reese, since it was something she had never done before. "I had a great time guest starring on *Friends*. The cast is so talented, they make what they do every day seem effortless," Reese said in an AOL online chat. "But I realized after being on the show how incredibly hard each one of them works every day. I was very impressed with their comedic timing and the way they work so well with each other."

Even though the character of Jill was materialistic, self-centered, and selfish, Reese gave her some heart and made her very funny and likeable. The two episodes she filmed were a hit, and the character of Jill was met with the seal of approval from *Friends* fans everywhere. There was talk of bringing Reese on for more episodes and even of giving Reese her very own show. Reese, however, was petrified of the live audience, and while she had been able to get past it for this short stint, she could not imagine doing it on a regular basis. "I love *Friends*—that is why I decided to do it. But when they asked me if I wanted to do my own show I thought, 'You know, I can't. I could never do it.' I had this total stage fright while I was there. I just froze," Reese told Jay Leno. "It was awful; it happened to me a lot. It's a live audience and I had never done anything in front of a live audience. And there's nothing worse than, like, telling a joke and it totally sucks and nobody laughs."

Coming off of *Friends*, Reese had once again proven that she was a comedic actress who could pull off a variety of characters and roles. It seemed like Jill had helped shake off some of the damage that Tracy Flick had done. Tracy had rubbed people the wrong way with her abrasive attitude and obnoxious need to succeed. People couldn't relate to her—instead, she turned them off and even scared them. Jill, on the other hand, was cute, bubbly, and friendly. Despite being spoiled and a little clueless, she was definitely someone you wanted to befriend and go on a shopping spree with. Everyone either knew someone like Jill or had a little bit of Jill in them. Reese had no choice but to take advantage of the new life that guest starring on *Friends* had breathed into her career, and find her next movie. Enter Elle Woods and a little movie called *Legally Blonde*.

11

Elle Woods Saves the Day

It's important to remember that, even though *Election* caused Reese to have some trouble getting into the right auditions and being first on the list with the right directors, it did earn her rave reviews and a Golden Globe nomination for Best Actress in a Musical or Comedy. So it was a mystery just what, exactly, was keeping Reese from moving on and finding her next part. Regardless, whatever that role ended up being, it had to be classy, it had to be light, it had to be memorable, and, most importantly, it had to take away whatever negativity *Election* had evoked. So when a script for a "chick flick" called *Legally Blonde* was sent her way, a lot of people in Reese's professional life told her not to even bother reading it. They thought it was a flip comedy with no depth and no merit and would essentially kill her career if it flopped—as they were certain it would. Reese, however, saw something more in the script and the character she would play and decided to take her chances.

Legally Blonde is about the ultimate California sorority girl, Elle Woods, who can't wait to graduate college and marry her boyfriend, Warner Huntington III. On the night she thinks he's going to propose, he breaks up with her instead, because he's going off to Harvard Law School and has decided that Elle isn't high-society enough for him. So, Elle uses her blissful ignorance and unwavering determination to literally charm her way into Harvard Law School, too, and get her boyfriend back. To everyone's surprise, she gets in; it turns out that Elle actually has a knack for the law, and she ends up a superstar on campus and in the courtroom, when she's able to get a fellow Delta Nu sorority sister off the hook from a murder charge.

Reese had read a lot of insipid girlfriend parts and was apprehensive until she read the script. While she knew she had to be careful about her next movie, there was something about Elle Woods that made Reese feel she had to play her. "I said, 'I don't know why, but I can do this. I have compassion for this person. I know who she is.' The part reminded me of those amazing Goldie Hawn movies I grew up watching, like *Private Benjamin* and *Overboard*, where everybody underestimates her, including herself, and then she has this great big comeuppance and becomes a better person through that journey. I completely related. There's no one like her. It's impossible to capture that kind of beautiful innocence with such intelligence underneath the surface," Reese told *Interview*. "When you look at Goldie's films, she seems ditzy in the beginning, but she always manages to turn everything on its ear. I actually watched Goldie and Gloria Steinem talking about her role in *Private Benjamin*, and that's what made me do it, when I heard Steinem talking about how important that role was for women to see, and how it was a great movie about how women can be underestimated."

With Goldie Hawn as her inspiration, Reese jumped headfirst into the role of Elle. Elle is bubbly, perky, always wears her favorite color—pink, takes her Chihuahua, Bruiser, with her wherever she goes, lives and breathes her sorority, and is an expert in all things shopping, dating, and partying. And of course, her signature trait is her perfect, sun-kissed blond hair. Reese wanted to make sure she nailed it perfectly, so, ever the "Little Miss Type A," she started doing her research. First stop? The University of Southern California. "I always do a lot of research out there for my roles because I think it's really important to observe the people that you are going to play. So for *Legally Blonde*, I went to the University of Southern California and was hanging out with the sorority girls. I think it's really important not to play the stereotypes you have in your head about what you think a character should be. I think it's really important to observe. And I've sort of slowly fancied myself and become this anthropologist who watches the way people walk and what they eat. And the vernacular they use and the way they relate to each other. I mean, do they hug when they meet, or do they kiss, or do they shake hands? And I try to incorporate all that sort of stuff into my work. And it really helps to put me into the shoes of the character and feel like I can take a little of myself out of it," Reese told *Star Interviews*. "And a lot of what I emerged with was that these woman are completely giving in their relationships with other women and completely supportive. And I think that really comes out in *Legally Blonde*. I mean, we really worked on it after a lot of the stuff we saw at USC and the sorority houses, and we incorporated a lot of that. Because there were some elements in the script before I went to USC of the women not being supportive of each other. And we thought, 'Well, that's such a great thing that you so rarely see in films, women having such a great camaraderie between the female characters.'"

With sorority life down pat, Reese's next stop was Neiman Marcus to get a better idea of what ladies who know their stuff when it comes to style, fashion, and shopping were like in their element. "Everyone thinks it's so funny I did research at Neiman Marcus, but I did! I think there's a really interesting culture in California, of women who go to lunch at these department stores, and meet their friends. And there's sort of a whole social structure. It's very interesting to me," Reese told *Star Interviews*. "It's really important not to put my own prejudices or my ideas about it, on the character I'm playing. It's just to be completely open. You know, as if you were that kind of person—how would you want to be represented?"

The last stop on Reese's research tour to make Elle Woods as true to life as possible was Loyola Law School. "It was really interesting. Very . . . well, I have to be honest, it was very tedious," Reese told *Star Interviews*. "It was just listening to a lot of jargon and that sort of thing. I think there was one blonde, in a whole class of 150 people. So you could see where Elle sticks out. And this was in California, too!"

As Reese finished researching her role, she started to love the optimistic and even misunderstood character of Elle, and it became an important labor of love for Reese to bring Elle to the masses in a memorable and charming way. While the movie could be seen as a bashing on blondes, it really was a love song to anyone—blonde, brunette, or redhead—who had ever been judged by their appearance. Reese could relate to playing a character riddled with stereotypes, as she had faced similar discrimination when she moved to Hollywood. "It was important to me not to ridicule blondes. When I first came to Hollywood I was not only blond, I was southern. And you know what that means," Reese told the *Tennessean*. "Elle is beautiful, rich, and seems to have everything. My challenge was to make her also likable. I wanted to break some clichés."

Reese also wanted to start appealing to a broader audience. "So many of the films that I did [up until *Legally Blonde*] have a very particular audience. And I just wanted to sort of broaden that. I also felt a responsibility to start speaking to my young female fans, because they are so easily influenced," Reese told *Star Interviews*. "I thought, 'This is such a great message for young women.' You know, about believing in yourself and following your dreams. And not being subservient to a relationship or other people's judgments of you."

The rest of the cast of *Legally Blonde* included a new actor named Matthew Davis, who plays her ex-boyfriend Warner; Selma Blair, with whom Reese had previously costarred in *Cruel Intentions*, plays Elle's fellow Harvard law classmate and Warner's new fiancé; Luke Wilson plays her law-professor-turned-love-interest; and Jennifer Coolidge plays Elle's frumpy friend, to whom she gives a complete makeover. This was the first movie where Reese was carrying the film on her shoulders, and she took that responsibility seriously. "This was the first movie where I was the lead, so it was a lot of hard work, but it was fun. There's a lot more pressure as far as the working hours are concerned. Some days I worked nineteen hours, and it was fifty-two days of shooting. And you certainly feel the pressure of carrying a film and making sure the cast is good—that everything goes smoothly. It's a lot of responsibility," Reese said in an AOL online chat. "I had a very good time in this movie. I enjoyed working with Selma Blair again. She and I are very close friends, so it was nice to be able to work with her again." Reese said she would put on Elle's high heels and instantly be in character. The director of *Legally Blonde*, Robert Luketic who was making his directorial debut, did not find Reese's commitment to the movie and the character as endearing as others did. If anything, he was turned off by how seriously Reese was taking the lighthearted and fun character of Elle. "Moviemaking is supposed to be fun. She would come out of her trailer and ask, 'Why are all of you laughing?' She

would want to know why we all had smiles on our faces," Luketic told
MSNBC.com. "Moviemaking to her is deadly serious business. There
is something impenetrable about that woman. I did not bond with
her." The rest of the cast had only glowing things to say about Reese,
and Reese herself had no idea that she had rubbed her director the
wrong way until he started speaking about it to the press. Reese told
Vanity Fair that she wished he had confronted her directly rather than
go behind her back and talk about it to the press.

Any drama on the set was quickly forgotten on July 13, 2001,
when *Legally Blonde* hit theaters. Reese held her breath. Though the
movie was a comedy and labeled a "chick flick," it was a real labor of
love for Reese. She had poured her heart and soul into developing Elle
Woods into something more than just a clueless blonde. The message
of the movie was meant to be inspiring and empowering to women
everywhere, and to make them believe that no matter who they are or
what they look like, and no matter how outlandish their dreams are,
anything they aspire to can come true. Because Reese was trying to
instill those same values in her own daughter, she was optimistic that
the film would be well received—she lived and breathed the philosophy behind *Legally Blonde*.

But the cultural phenomenon that swept the United States that
weekend was nothing that anyone, not even Reese, could have
predicted.

Legally Blonde opened at number one and ended up grossing over
$141 million worldwide. That fan base of young women that Reese so
badly wanted to reach out to was suddenly at her beck and call. While
Hollywood appreciated Reese's performance in *Election* as Tracy Flick
but couldn't stand the thought of working with Reese just in case she
was Tracy Flick . . . *Legally Blonde* had exactly the opposite effect.

Hollywood raved about Reese's performance as Elle, and all of Hollywood was clamoring to work with her. After all, who wouldn't want to work with the captivating and enchanting Elle Woods? As one particularly standout review by Stephen Hunter from the *Washington Post* said of Reese's performance, "We know what smart people look like. And they don't look like Elle Woods. Her hair a froth of cornsilk. Her eyes as blue as blue can get. Sparkly, too. Perched on tiny pink toes in her hip mules, her pixie nose upturned like Tinker Bell's, her waist a tiny isthmus, her bust luxuriant, her face not merely beautiful but lively, curious, animated, perfected then amplified in its beauty by makeup so skillfully applied Rembrandt must have done it, a little slice of *el primo*. It's to Witherspoon's greater glory as an actress that she's able to show us the doubleness of Elle, and make us care for her so deeply. Witherspoon is too good for the rickety obviousness in which she's marooned; in the hands of some lesser blonde—God help us, an Alicia Silverstone or even a Sarah Michelle Gellar—the thinness of the material would wear us down."

Elle Woods' optimism and brightness turned around Reese's status in Hollywood literally overnight. Reese's manager called her after the weekend box office results came out to tell her that she was on the short list of every director and casting director in town. To put it simply: everyone suddenly wanted, no, needed, to have Reese attached to their projects. Reese was overwhelmed. "I didn't even know there was such a thing as a short list. It seems my manager never told me about it because she didn't want me to be disappointed that I wasn't on it," Reese told *Entertainment Weekly*. "I can feel comfortable now. After twelve years in the business, it seems I am an overnight sensation."

The attraction to *Legally Blonde* involved the deeper stories the film told about finding yourself, proving your critics wrong, and discovering that a man alone won't fulfill your life. Young girls and women all over the country just couldn't get enough, and Reese was thrilled by how empowered they were feeling after seeing the film. "I think this movie has a great message in that sense, I mean Elle is just so myopic. She's just so driven. And she almost seems completely unaware that people are thinking such terrible things about her, until that big moment when she says to her boyfriend: 'I'm not good enough for you, am I?' And I just think it's really important to keep a focus, you know. And try not to concentrate on the bad things. So a lot of the positivity of this character has worn off on me!" Reese told *Star Interviews*.

Reese became an unofficial spokesperson for women everywhere, encouraging them to follow in Elle's footsteps and depend on themselves to feel complete and satisfied. "In the beginning of the movie, Elle is not an independent woman at all. I mean her whole life and her whole self-worth is derived from her ex-boyfriend's opinions of her. And I love that idea. Because I saw, especially growing up, so many girls involved in these relationships that were like little pseudomarriages. And they put so much self-worth into what these men think about them," Reese told *Star Interviews*. "I thought that was a really valuable message to young women—it's great if you can have a good, healthy relationship. But don't throw away your dreams over some relationship that's just detrimental to your future. And you have to really seek out your potential. Like, relationships aren't the end-all, be-all. Be all of who you are when you're twenty-two. Wait, I say that and I was married at twenty-three! But I feel like I've had a healthy relationship with Ryan, so it's different."

Life changed for Reese. Her career had rebooted with the release of *Legally Blonde*, and suddenly she had to adjust to the heightened interest in her personal life and a more demanding professional schedule. "I'm more surprised than anyone [that *Legally Blonde* was a success]. I knew it was a good film when I read the script. Or, I should say, I knew it would be a good film when I read the script, but I had no idea audiences would love it as much as they do," Reese told an AOL online chat.

With so many people trying to pull Reese into so many different directions, she had to be careful about whom she could let in and whom she could trust. The one thing she was grateful for was the people she already had surrounding her before her career skyrocketed. "I feel very lucky to have friends in my life who knew me before *Legally Blonde*," Reese told *InStyle*. "I value my friends' honesty and my husband's honesty." With Elle Woods as Reese's ticket to the next level of fame, there was no stopping her career as a bona fide A-list Hollywood actress.

Two months after *Legally Blonde* was released in theaters, on September 11, 2001, the innocence of Elle Woods seemed to be lost in America. After the devastating events of that day, when four commercial airplanes were hijacked and the World Trade Center was attacked, it seemed as if America might never again enjoy a movie or be able to laugh and have fun. The mood of the country was somber, and the feeling was that there were bigger things happening in the world than seemingly frivolous things like TV, movies, and music. But after the shock of September 11 started to wear off, it became apparent that what America needed was to move on and heal. The best way to do that was with laughter and quality entertainment. So the first major television event after September 11 was the twenty-seventh season premiere of *Saturday Night Live*. Since the show is an institution in the city of New York, where it is filmed, and since New York was hit the hardest during the attacks, it was imperative that *SNL* let people know

that it was OK to laugh again. And who better to host that pivotal
show than the summer's brightest new star—Reese Witherspoon. It
was refreshing and comforting to the American public to know that
Reese was taking on this delicate job. They trusted her to make them
laugh, and Reese took that responsibility very seriously.

On September 29, 2001, *Saturday Night Live* opened with New
York City's mayor Rudy Giuliani and *SNL* creator Lorne Michaels
announcing that New York City was officially back up and running,
before Paul Simon performed an emotional rendition of "The Boxer."
Reese then came onstage for her all-important opening monologue,
which was sweet, simple, and memorable in this emotional and nerve-
wracking time in history. Reese's monologue went like this:

"Thank you. I'm so happy and honored to be here tonight, and,
most of all, I'm happy that you all are here with me. We've never done
a show under these circumstances, so we're still finding our way. But
I promise you that we're gonna give it everything we've got. So, this
is the part of the show where the host usually says something funny,
but I don't know any jokes. I know one joke, but it has a bad word in
it, so I probably shouldn't tell it, should I? [audience eggs her on to tell
the joke anyway] OK—you asked for it. Here it goes: There's this
polar bear couple, and they have this beautiful polar bear baby. And
they're so happy, they can't believe it, he's just the cutest, sweetest
polar bear cub. And he learns to run really fast, and he learns to talk
early, and the first question he asks his mother is, 'Mom? Am I a real
polar bear?' And his mother says, 'Yes, you're a real polar bear. I'm a
polar bear, and your daddy's a polar bear, so of course, you're a polar
bear.' So the baby polar bear is growing stronger every day, and he
learns to fish before any of the other baby polar bears, and his parents
are just really proud of him. And after a few months, the baby polar

bear comes up to his mom and asks, 'Mom, are you sure I'm pure polar bear?' And his mother says, 'Yes, honey, we're polar bears. Your grandma and grandpa are polar bears. You're pure polar bear.' And he says, 'OK.' Then, on the baby polar bear's first birthday, his parents throw him a huge party, and all the polar bears come, because they love him so much, and as the baby polar bear is about to blow out the candles on his cake, he turns to his mother and he asks, 'Mom, are you sure I'm 100 percent pure polar bear?' 'Yes, you are 100 percent pure polar bear. But why do you keep asking me that?' And the baby polar bear says, 'Because I'm freezing my balls off!' So, that's my joke! Alicia Keys is here to help us have a good time. So stick around and see what happens!"

12

A Rocky Romance

Reese Witherspoon had made seventeen movies and had been acting for almost ten years, but it was not until she stepped into an all-pink wardrobe and became the perkiest lawyer in the bar association that she became a star. That post–September 11 *Saturday Night Live* represented one of the first events that started to take the American public's minds off the tragic events and start looking to the future. As for Reese, life after *Legally Blonde* was released was good, and it made things even better to have the unwavering support of her husband and daughter to keep her grounded and remind her that there were more important things in life than fame.

Reese and Ryan had now been married for three years, and the relationship was strong. They had come to really lean on each other and missed each other immensely when they were apart. "He makes me much calmer. I fret a lot about decisions I make. And he'll be the one to say, 'Honey, it's just a movie. It's three months out of our lives. If it stresses you out, maybe you ought to let it go,'" Reese told *Good Housekeeping*. "He's a good influence on me because he's so grounded. I think it helps, too, that we were both so young when we met so we've grown a lot together. It's weird—when I met him, I just knew: this is the guy for me. He's so smart and, honestly, that's a big thing for me. You've got to know what's going on and he knows more than I do, which is a big deal."

On the set of *Legally Blonde*, Ryan came by to visit Reese before heading out to the set of a movie he was filming out of town. Reese was overcome with emotion at the thought of them being apart and started to cry. The cast and crew were touched by the sweet way Ryan calmed Reese down and made sure she was OK before he left. Reese's *Legally Blonde* costar Jennifer Coolidge was particularly moved by the scene and the sweet words that Ryan said to Reese. "Reese was crying in the driveway and Ryan said, 'Why are you crying? You're going to see me for the rest of your life.' I mean, what girl wouldn't want to hear that?" Jennifer recalled to *Vanity Fair*. And while Reese's star was surpassing Ryan's, who had yet to have another hit since *Cruel Intentions*, he looked nothing but proud of his wife whenever they were in public together and the attention was clearly on Reese. One funny moment occurred when they attended a red carpet event together; Reese was decked out from head to toe, with her hair and makeup sparkling and a designer dress fitting to a T. The paparazzi were going crazy trying to get the perfect shot of Reese. Ryan was, of course, by her side, but he was so dressed down in comparison with Reese that security assumed he was a fan overstepping his bounds. They told Ryan to step back and said that if he wanted an autograph, he was going to have to stop crowding Miss Witherspoon. The fact that they could put up with such misunderstandings was a testament to their strong marriage. Many guys would not be able to handle their wife being more successful, but Ryan seemed to be taking it all in stride.

In December 2001, *Gosford Park*, a Robert Altman period piece that Ryan was honored to be in, was released. It was his moment to shine again, though it was a different role for Ryan than anything he had ever played before; it was more mature and a far cry from the teen genre that had made him famous. The film was by no means a box office smash, but it was critically acclaimed and nominated for numerous Oscars, including Best Picture. It was an absolute coup that Ryan had landed a role in an ensemble cast with accomplished British actors such as Helen Mirren and Maggie Smith. Even with such great buzz surrounding the film, however, it did not raise Ryan's profile the way that *Legally Blonde* had catapulted Reese into another level of fame. And that's when the world started to speculate that maybe things weren't exactly perfect between Reese and Ryan. Unfounded rumors that their marriage was on the rocks started to swirl, and the tabloids reported that it was because Reese had suddenly become a lot more famous and Ryan was unable to handle the imbalance in their careers. Reese and Ryan didn't respond to the rumors and laughed them off. But then, at the Academy Awards in March 2002, one comment suddenly thrust their relationship into the spotlight.

Reese and Ryan came out onstage to present the award for Best Makeup. When it was time to reveal the winner, Reese playfully asked Ryan if she could announce the name. Ryan said, "You make more money than I do—go ahead." There was uncomfortable laughter from the audience, and afterward the press began prying into their personal lives to a degree they had never quite experienced before. The press was convinced that that comment alluded to bigger issues with ego and jealousy between the two of them, and when the press thinks there is a story to tell, there is no stopping their digging around to get it. Reese was shocked that the press was making such a big deal of the comment and said on the record that it was just a display of Ryan's sense of humor. "It was our way of bringing to light an issue that everyone has been talking about behind our backs as if we don't know about it. I thought it was the perfect way to let the world know that, 'Yes, we know about this, too!'" Reese told WENN. "It really doesn't matter to us. He's incredibly supportive of me, as I am of him. We work as a team, and the bottom line about the money issue is that it's part of our job. What's really important to both of us isn't who earns how much, but how we get along with each other within the family. And we get along just fine." Reese went on to explain to *InStyle*, "It shows how comfortable he is with it. The next day it'll be him making more money than me. You're up; you're down; but no matter what, we're together."

Then Ryan casually mentioned in an interview that he and Reese regularly went to couples' therapy. He might as well have said that their relationship was on thin ice—which it was not at all—and the press joined the fact that they were in therapy with Ryan's snide comment at the Oscars, concluding that their marriage was almost over. "I feel like that whole thing got misconstrued. People were not nice about it. They thought it connoted this big dark cloud on our lives. Since when is self-improvement a negative? Why wouldn't I be interested in psychology? I like to read psychology books. I'm obsessed with child behavior; I would love to be a child psychologist," Reese said in their defense to *Vanity Fair*. "Ryan is literally my best friend. He makes me laugh; he makes me think about things. We're both actors, so we can commiserate about the bad things and celebrate the good aspects of it. It's a great friendship and I feel really blessed to have a great friend as my love." Reese was upset that her marriage was being subjected to so much scrutiny. The equal partnership they shared was something she was proud of, and she resented that anyone would dare question it. "I think things are changing. A lot of young married people grew up in dual-income homes and had mothers who worked. The men are much more involved with child care. With my husband it's fifty-fifty," Reese said to *Vanity Fair*. "We've never been competitive with each other. Ryan is very successful. He gets tons of offers every month for tons of money. We're talking enormous sums of money, yet people think it's not important because it's not as much as me. By anyone's standards, Ryan is *more* than successful."

The truth of the matter was that Reese and Ryan had started going to therapy to avoid falling into the Hollywood cliché that high-profile marriages were doomed. Since both Reese's and Ryan's parents were still together and going strong, they had a lot to live up to, and they knew that it was going to take work whether they were famous or not. "Marriage is hard. I think the greatest lesson I could take from my parents' marriage or Ryan's parents' marriage is to go with the flow. You think you can't get over certain things, and you do. You only learn that through sticking with it," Reese told *Vanity Fair*. "I had a real good idea of what a working marriage relationship is. It's not about expecting someone to make you happy every day or to complete your life. It's a great partnership. Two individuals come together and share a life, have children, and hopefully you come out of it friends. I never thought it was easy. I still don't think it's easy." And the fact that both Reese and Ryan recognized that marriage wasn't easy is what led them to therapy in the first place. "I think if anybody rests on the idea that they are perfect or their life is perfect or their relationship is perfect and is so troubled about destroying the facade as opposed to getting to what's real—that is troublesome," Reese told *Interview*. "Who is so arrogant and vain that they don't want people to know they're real or human?

That they're fallible? We are all just people. That's part of what's amazing about being an actor. It's about compassion and deep feeling for other people's pain or struggle or drive. I never feel above them. I never feel beneath them. That's probably what led me to this profession."

13

Home Sweet Home

Throughout the rest of 2002, Reese continued to ride high on the success of *Legally Blonde* and refused to let the rumors about her marriage affect her life and the way she was living it. She was enjoying being a mother to Ava and was looking forward to making more movies. Reese decided to follow up *Legally Blonde* with a remake of *The Importance of Being Earnest* based on the famous Oscar Wilde play about two friends who use the pseudonym "Earnest" just for kicks—until they each fall in love while posing as Earnest, and a case of mistaken identity ensues. Since it was a period piece, Reese had to perfect an English accent. "I hadn't done a lot of period stuff, and I saw it as a challenge. It was a good way to initiate myself to a foreign accent but not have the lead in the film," Reese told *Vanity Fair*. "I worked really hard, because, you know, you can sink or swim in these situations."

It was an interesting household, because Ryan was learning a Scottish accent for his role in the movie *Gosford Park*. He nailed it right away, while Reese had to keep practicing. Funnily enough, it was little Ava who wound up surprising her parents by picking up both accents flawlessly. It was, however, a challenge for Reese to get the dialect just right. "I had to work like a dog to get that accent down. Three hours a day for six weeks. Not only that, but I had to come back weeks later and redub almost everything, because nobody apparently had noticed there was a very noisy airport near the elegant manor where the movie was shot," Reese told the *Tennessean*. "The most enervating thing about it was hearing my husband pick up a Scottish accent in only about three days. I know the studio people were pretty shaky about me doing the accent. I hope I didn't disappoint them."

Learning the accent was even more stressful due to the fact that Reese was practically the only American in the largely British cast, which included esteemed actors like Dame Judi Dench, Frances O'Connor, Colin Firth, and Rupert Everett. Being around an Oscar-winning actress like Judi Dench was particularly stressful. "I worked with a dialect coach three hours a day for six weeks. And I really struggled. I cannot express to you how difficult it was!" Reese recalled to *Glamour* in their UK edition. "Then came the day I had to walk out on the set and do it in front of Judi Dench! When I saw the film, I couldn't even watch without thinking, 'That's me with a funny voice!'" Her costars and the director of the film, Oliver Parker, were particularly impressed with having Reese Witherspoon as part of the cast. "Absolutely [it's daunting for Witherspoon]. It's a very daunting prospect, slotting into this thing, which is, on the whole, a very British possession, and to come in as an outsider, especially when you are surrounded by the likes of Judi Dench," Parker explained to *Vanity Fair*. "But Reese is a terrific little impressionist. She works like crazy and she is meticulous—something of a perfectionist. I don't think she would have taken *The Importance of Being Earnest* on unless she thought she could get there." Her costar Frances O'Connor seconded that when she told *Vanity Fair* that "Reese is not pretending to be anything she is not and I think that's really refreshing. She came up with the goods." When it came down to it, Parker couldn't envision anyone *but* Reese playing the role of Cecily. "Cecily is one of the trickier parts to cast because very often it can be an irritating character. It's meant to have a youthfulness and strength, but usually you get someone too old. This is a sweet young thing, but the more you get to know her, the more you realize there's really a tenacious, wise creature in there," he told *Vanity Fair*. "There are very few actors Reese's age with that sort of maturity. You've got to have someone who has sort of a blazing intelligence without showing it off. And Reese is extremely smart."

The Importance of Being Earnest was not exactly a box office hit, and the reviews, especially for Reese, were not the most favorable. But it was such a small release that it came and went so fast that no one even realized Reese had another movie in theaters. And it didn't matter, because just four months later, in September 2002, Reese released a movie called *Sweet Home Alabama* that would strengthen her star power in ways she did not think possible. Very few female actresses can be a sure thing to open a movie, especially a romantic comedy like *Sweet Home Alabama*. At the time, Julia Roberts and Cameron Diaz were two of the biggest, and even they weren't quite the sure things they used to be. But with the success of *Legally Blonde*, followed by the enormous success of *Sweet Home Alabama*, it looked like Reese was poised to join the club.

In *Sweet Home Alabama*, Reese played Melanie Carmichael, a hot, young, in-demand New York fashion designer who gets engaged to Andrew Hennings (played by *Grey's Anatomy*'s Dr. McDreamy, Patrick Dempsey), the son of New York City's mayor and the hottest bachelor in town. She becomes the most envied girl in New York when he proposes to her inside the famed Fifth Avenue Tiffany's store and then tells her that she can choose any ring she desires. (That scene became an instant classic and one of the most memorable proposals in movie history.) Melanie accepts his proposal but doesn't realize that first she has to go back home to Alabama to a life she left behind to divorce her childhood sweetheart Jake (played by Josh Lucas). The only problem is that Jake refuses to divorce her—forcing her new New York life and her former southern life to collide. "The idea of going to a different environment and making it and then going back home, having to keep up two personas—all of that was very personal to me," Reese told *InStyle*. But she was excited to go back to what she knew best—life in the South. "It was great to get back to my southern roots," she told *People*. "I think people can tell when you're having fun in a movie."

Sweet Home Alabama reunited Reese with director Andy Tennant, who had last worked with Reese when she was just a teenager in one of her very first projects, a made-for-TV movie called *Desperate Choices: To Save My Child*. It was a happy reunion, as Andy and Reese had mutual respect for each other. "When I found out Andy wrote this and was going to direct it, I was excited, because we had such a good time working with each other," Reese told *FilmStew*. "He's such a fun guy and he also really understands female characters. For some reason, he just has incredible insight into the female psyche and understands women, and not in an overly sappy or saccharine way. He just understands the practical issues that women deal with." Tennant echoed the sentiment about Reese, telling *InStyle*, "Working with Reese is like playing doubles tennis: you know she's got her half of the court covered."

Reese had always been in consideration for the role of Melanie, but she initially had some competition and it wasn't a sure thing that she was going to get the part. Then, the weekend after *Legally Blonde* opened, there was no one else anyone working on the film could imagine playing Melanie other than Reese. Tennant went to her with the script and was ecstatic and relieved that she liked it so much that she accepted the role. "After *Man in the Moon*, and then some other things, Reese was a dramatic actress girl. We'd chat occasionally and then I went to see *Election* and I was like, 'She's funny, wow, she's a goof!' It was almost a caricature of a performance," Andy told *FilmStew*. "And then *Legally Blonde* came out and was another big, over-the-top comedy, but I knew her this other way. *Sweet Home Alabama* was a really good opportunity to take both of those talents and have her do something a little more real."

Even though the movie took place in New York City and Alabama, they filmed mainly in Atlanta, Georgia. Reese, Ryan, and Ava moved into an apartment there while she was filming. Tennant was amazed at how easily she balanced her professional obligations with her personal life. He recalled one particular example to *Vanity Fair*. "We were working long days, and Reese and I lived in the same apartment building in Georgia. I was waiting for the elevator one Sunday morning, and I hear this scream from hell emanating from somewhere in the building—I mean, it's just awful. As the elevator arrives, the sound gets louder. Then the doors open, and there is Reese, at 7:30 in the morning, trying to balance a Starbucks with a screaming baby and two bags of groceries. She has herself and the coffee pinned against the wall and she just smiles at me and says 'Hi!' Then the doors close and up she goes."

It was all in a day's work for Reese, and she was committed to playing Melanie because she could very much relate to her. "The reason I decided to do this film was that it was very personal for me. I've been playing a lot of characters that were larger than life and very kinetic. When I read this, it reminded me of my own sort of things that I went through, coming from Nashville and moving to Los Angeles and rejecting my past for a stint and then, having to come back and figure out which parts of it were important to my identity," Reese told *Film-Stew*. "We talked a lot about [the way the South would be portrayed in the film]. My main concern was that it not represent southern people in a way I grew up watching southern people being portrayed in movies, which was basically as ignorant and inbred. And I wanted to celebrate the eccentricities of southern people because there is a lot of humor there, but also represent the values and morals that they have." Reese was also very drawn to Melanie because she was so real, and Reese could relate to her in ways she had not been able to relate to some of her other characters. "She's similar to how I see myself. I realized it had been quite some time since I had played a person that was recognizable as not a caricature—just a normal girl," Reese told *W*. "I needed to reconnect with myself as an actress, to show a little bit of myself by being a girl that's the closest to my real life, in the sense of her upbringing and her heritage." Because Reese could relate to Melanie and found that she hit closer to home, she actually found it a more challenging role to play. "It's almost harder for me to do a role like Melanie in *Sweet Home Alabama* where I'm using more of own real voice," she told *What*. "That's more challenging to me than, say, playing a Tracy Flick. That kind of role is also a lot of work, but I feel more naturally inclined to play off-the-wall roles that are sort of larger than life. It's fun."

If Reese had any doubts or apprehensions about playing Melanie, it was news to her costars, who loved working with her because they learned so much from watching her commitment to the character and the movie. "The thing about Reese is that she's massively intelligent and she knows her job like the back of her hand. She comes in with a level of preparation that is awesome," Josh Lucas told *FilmStew*. "A lot of my responsibility was to react off of where she was going and trust her instincts, knowing that I've seen them enough to know that they're so much better than mine. I think that worked best for me—to not have to drive it at all." Reese's other leading man, Patrick Dempsey, was simply enchanted by the presence she commanded without even trying on set. "I don't know what it is, but there is something magical about her. The camera loves her. She has a lot of depth and strength of character and I think that translates into the characters that she plays," he told *FilmStew*. "They're strong and edgy, interesting women. I think that is part of the appeal. I think that women love that about her and men find that really attractive. She has that indefinable something—that movie-star quality."

The success of *Sweet Home Alabama* was another notch on Reese's belt of achievements as a true powerhouse in Hollywood. She was a sure thing at the box office, which led her to create her own production company, called Type A Productions. Many thought she'd chosen the name because of her childhood nickname, "Little Miss Type A," but that was actually not the case. "People think I named it after myself . . . but it just isn't who I am at all. It was actually an in-joke with my family, because at seven I understood complicated medical terms, such as the difference between type A and type B personalities," Reese told *Interview*. "But I just wished I'd named the company Dogfood Films or Fork or something. You carry that baggage all your life."

Regardless of the name, the company gave Reese even more power, and the freedom to create projects for herself as well as other young actors and actresses that she was passionate about and proud to release. Her first project was to go back to the character that had changed her life and career, and bring Elle Woods back to the big screen. Reese and Type A Productions were going to executive-produce a sequel to *Legally Blonde* called *Legally Blonde 2: Red, White and Blonde*. Reese was also about to make history by earning a $22 million paycheck to star in the sequel. She was in the club of actresses who made over $20 million per film that was limited to the likes of Julia Roberts and Cameron Diaz. In January 2003, right as Reese was about to start filming, she topped an *Entertainment Weekly* reader poll of their top ten favorite actresses. She led the pack with Renee Zellweger second in the poll, followed by Nicole Kidman in third place, Julia Roberts in fourth, Julianne Moore in fifth, Halle Berry in sixth, Kirsten Dunst in seventh, Jennifer Lopez in eighth, Cameron Diaz in ninth, and Drew Barrymore in tenth. Reese was no longer just a star—she was a superstar.

Despite being one of the biggest celebrities in the world, Reese was kept grounded by her family—especially her family back home in Nashville. Reese hadn't let her close-knit relationship with her family diminish since she'd moved to Los Angeles to become a star. In fact, while Reese was filming *Sweet Home Alabama*, she hired her brother, John, to be her chauffeur. Reese's family was her rock, and they were who she turned to for a sense of normalcy after a long day of shooting or walking the red carpet. Reese was also extremely protective of her family and was not happy to hear that the paparazzi had figured out where her parents' home in Nashville was located and staked it out for pictures and information about Reese. What made the paparazzi's discovery of her family's whereabouts even harder for Reese was that her brother John had gone through a very difficult and troubling time, and she did not want this information to be leaked to the press or made into a big deal, for his sake as well as her own.

John had a problem with alcohol long before Reese was a star, and in October 2002, his problems took a turn when he was arrested in Nashville after a woman accused him of attacking her inside her home. He was charged with sexual battery and aggravated burglary but was released after posting a $24,000 bond.

It was shocking for Reese to hear of her brother sinking just as she was rising to the top of her career. The details were unbearable—John had entered his neighbor's home and started undressing the woman inside who was asleep on the couch; he was so inebriated, he thought he was in his own home. He admitted through his lawyer that he was sure it was a mistake brought on by a bout of drunkenness. To make matters worse, only the weekend before, John had been arrested for an outstanding warrant for a DUI in May 2001. A year later, when the sexual assault case went to trial, John pled guilty and, as part of his plea, had to attend weekly meetings at Nashville's Vanderbilt Institute for the Treatment of Addiction for at least the next two years. The news of John's arrest, drinking problems, and legal woes never made national headlines, but Reese was adamant about keeping his situation private—even to those reporters who did know about it and felt they had to ask Reese about it. In 2004, Reese told *Vanity Fair* that John's troubles were his business. "I feel guilty because of my success, people seem to have opinions about people in my life," she said. "I feel responsible for their lives being in a fishbowl. We're not the Kennedys. We don't have a public responsibility. We're just regular folks, trying to do the best we can. People make mistakes. Alcoholism is a terrible disease and it's affected my family in lots of ways, for generations."

14

Baby Makes Four

Reese was excited to step back into the kitten heels of Elle Woods and bring her back to the big screen. In the two years since the first movie had come out, Reese's life had changed drastically, but the one thing she loved most was the little girls who came up to her and told her how much Elle Woods inspired them in their own lives. "I got a lot of great things, like six-year-olds saying, 'I want to go to Harvard Law School!'" Reese told *People*. "It's so inspiring to me as a woman." She went on to explain just what it was about Elle that made her so special. "Part of what I love about Elle is she's fun. She's laughing and she's girlie and she likes to have her nails done. But she is also successful and ambitious. She's not just what you think she is."

The second chapter of Elle Woods' life takes place right after she graduates from Harvard Law School. Reese described the inspiration for the sequel as *"Mr. Smith Goes to Washington*, but from a female perspective." In *Legally Blonde 2*, Elle wants her Chihuahua, Bruiser, to reunite with his mother, because she would like Bruiser's mother to be in attendance at her wedding. When she discovers that Bruiser's mom is a test animal for a cosmetics company, she leaves Boston to move to

Washington, D.C., to convince Congress to ban all animal testing, but she has very little luck and, of course, all of her co-workers and members of Congress have a hard time taking a perky blonde with a perfect pink wardrobe seriously. Eventually she wins them over—with the help of her former Delta Nu sorority sisters, of course—and gets the ban passed.

Returning to the cast besides Luke was Jennifer Coolidge, who plays her best friend Paulette, and Jessica Cauffiel and Alanna Ubach as her sorority sisters who are always there for Elle in a pinch. New to the cast was legendary comedian and actor Bob Newhart, who plays Elle's doorman, with the inside scoop on everyone in town, and Oscar-winning actress Sally Field, who plays a two-faced congresswoman Elle works with in D.C.

When filming on *Legally Blonde 2* began, the set was lively and fun. While the first movie had been directed by Robert Luketic, who went on the record to say that he did not enjoy working with Reese, the second was directed by Charles Herman-Wurmfeld, who had directed the independent film *Kissing Jessica Stein*, a surprise hit. He had nothing but glowing things to say about the energy on the set and how Reese made the cast feel right at home. "She showered us with cookies and ice cream," he told *People*. "She also brought in a karaoke machine and serenaded the crew with Dolly Parton's '9 to 5.'" This time around, Reese had a bigger stake in the movie than just being the lead—she was also the boss, as she was executive producer, a responsibility she took seriously despite making sure there were fun things to do off camera. "When the studio came to me, I said, 'Well, I have so many ideas about this, I have to be involved from the very beginning.' I think Elle is such a great role model for young women, in the sense that she's girlie and frivolous—but she's still ambitious and wants to be successful. And smart in her own way, too," Reese told *Marie Claire*. "So we came up with an idea for a sequel, and then I became involved in everything! I had to work with the writers because when it's so much about that one character, it's so important that her integrity is maintained throughout the script—that she doesn't say a line that's false or have a pessimistic moment. So [being executive producer] is really about bringing the characters to life." Getting back into the world of Elle Woods was nothing but fun for Reese. The only problem was her hair, which was still short from *Sweet Home Alabama*. Elle, of course, has flowing blond locks. So, all of Elle's hairstyles throughout the movie were top-grade wigs!

Marc Platt, who was a producer on the first movie, was back as Reese's coproducer; and he was happy for Reese and her success since the first movie. "She has matured as she's taken on the responsibility of being a movie star and raising a family," he told *People*. "She's a little more serious, although still a lot of fun." Sally Field, a veteran of the industry, was equally as impressed by Reese as her boss and Reese the actress. "We had a lot of long talks about everything," Sally told *People*. "She is a serious actress. She's very curious, and she really wants to know what other people have been through."

As excitement started to build for the release of the movie, which was slated for the July 4 weekend of 2003, Mattel even released an Elle Woods Barbie to commemorate the sequel and the strong woman that Elle represented to Barbie fans everywhere. Reese was very excited—especially since the only Barbie she had bought Ava up until that point was a President of the United States Barbie. Reese felt that now that Ava's mom was a Barbie herself, she could have that one, too. There's even a line in *Legally Blonde 2* where Elle is referred to as "Capitol Hill Barbie."

While waiting for *Legally Blonde 2: Red, White and Blonde* to hit theaters, Reese signed on for the movie adaptation of William Makepeace
Thackeray's book *Vanity Fair*, to be directed by acclaimed film director
Mira Nair of *Monsoon Wedding* fame. Reese had been calling Nair for
more than two years, trying to get her to direct one of her projects.
"When we finally sat down, we really hit it off," Reese told the *Independent*. "I really admire her visual sensibility and also her sense of
character. There are no good guys or bad guys in her movies, they're
all just very real portraits of human behavior."

So when Nair wanted Reese to play social climber Becky Sharp in
Vanity Fair, Reese could not say no—and Nair wasn't going to let the
movie be made without Reese as her Becky. "I saw Reese in *Election*
and I knew she could play Becky. She's a movie star. She commands the
camera. She's very natural in front of it," Nair told the *Virginian*. "I'm
not interested in making a typical period movie. Becky is a very
modern woman—making her way. It was entirely appropriate that
Reese is the only American in the cast. Becky, after all, is an outsider.
An orphan, she is the lowest in society in a world that buys and sells
people by their rank and position. Every modern woman will admire
her and her methods."

Reese, Ava, and Ryan packed their bags and moved to London,
where the film was going to be shot. As Reese prepared for her part,
Nair kept telling her that she actually needed to gain weight to play the
sensual Becky Sharp. "Mira's the first director I ever met who, when
she met me, she goes, 'Mmmm, you're going to need to gain some
weight.' I was like, 'I love you. I love you. Who are you?'" Reese told
CBS's *Early Show*. "She's like, 'Yes. You need to look much more voluptuous.' Then she turns to Ryan and says, 'I think it's time for her to
get pregnant.'" Nair really wanted her and Reese's version to be a

"full-blown sensual woman" as Nair told *Vanity Fair* magazine; the problem was that it was hard for Nair to get Reese to flaunt what she had. "When Mira starts talking about bosoms and having flesh, I start to sweat," Reese admitted to *Vanity Fair*. "There's something about overt sexuality . . . like it's scatological or something! I'm all about trying to make movies that have nothing to do with my body. I'm prudish and nervous. I don't have the excuse that my grandmother is watching anymore, but she's watching [from heaven]. It makes me nervous when I see a woman with her midriff showing. I would never do that on purpose, and if it happened by accident I'd be mortified! I feel threatened by women who are on the cover of hootchie-kootchie magazines!"

In a most interesting turn of events, just as shooting was about to begin, Reese discovered that she and Ryan were indeed about to expand their family with a baby due in late 2003, so her body was going to be voluptuous whether Reese was comfortable with it or not. "I got my wish!" Nair told *Vanity Fair*. Even though Nair wanted that look for the part, in the book, Becky was not pregnant, and there was going to be no way to hide Reese's expanding stomach throughout filming. So, Nair being the visionary that she is, she decided there was nothing wrong with Becky Sharp being pregnant in her version of the story and rewrote the part to incorporate that plot twist just for Reese. "I am a real believer in full-blown sensuality," Nair told *Vanity Fair*. And Reese was fully comfortable with Nair's vision. "The thing about working with Mira Nair is that she has this way of putting sexuality in her films in a way that's not gratuitous," she told the *National Post*. "It's not overt. It's very much female sensuality."

With a second *Legally Blonde* on the verge of hitting theaters, taking a part in a period piece after having so much commercial success seemed like an odd choice for Reese. But to her, it made perfect sense on her career trajectory. "I was coming off of movies like *Legally Blonde 1* and *2*, but Mira was still saying, 'No, no, Reese is the woman to do this classic piece of literature in a highly dramatic film,'" Reese told the *National Post*. "I mean, just saying that and putting me out there was a really huge vote of confidence that made me feel like I could do it." And while Reese loved the lighthearted films she was famous for, it was time to grow as an actress, too. "I was excited [to play Becky Sharp]. I do films like *Legally Blonde* and *Sweet Home Alabama* because I love those performances and doing films that people can take their kids to and leave feeling happy. But in the times where I'm trying to challenge myself and do roles that aren't about making a lot of money or aren't about feeding a big commercial audience, I try to do something very different. I was surprised that the *Vanity Fair* character came off so sympathetic," Reese told *Flare*. "Playing the younger parts are harder because I just don't feel that young anymore. The older parts are easier for me to understand because I feel a lot older than I am. I have lived a lot and have a lot of experiences." Nair, for her part, could not think of any actress who was better suited for the role than Reese. "Thackeray describes Becky as minxlike, and that's so much Reese. In her eyes, as in Becky Sharp's, five or six things can go on, clickety-clack, at the same time," Nair told the *Independent*. "Also, I wanted to see a girl like Reese, who is always offered cute girl parts, as a really full-blown womanly creature . . . I couldn't think of another actress who could play from seventeen to thirty-five with the maturity of Reese."

Being pregnant did prove challenging, even with it being written into the script. Reese's stomach was expanding faster than filming could keep up with, but thankfully the costumes of that era included high-waisted and loose-fitting gowns. Reese was more tired than usual, as well, but she found the motivation to keep going. "I was very pregnant during filming and working eighteen hours a day. But I'd look around at Mira, who's a mother, and the other producers, who are women with children, and I'd think, I can do this," Reese told *InStyle*. She tried not to let her pregnancy slow her down or prohibit her from anything she was expected to do. "I thought it was rather brave of Reese to do a [love] scene," her costar, James Purefoy, told the *Record*. "When I touch Reese's stomach, that's not a prosthetic, that was a baby in there." Reese's dedication was noticed by everyone she worked with on the movie. "She'd give a megawatt smile after twelve-hour shoots in damp English mansions," Nair told *InStyle*.

Filming the movie while she was pregnant was worth it to Reese. She had her family with her, and London was a town that Reese and Ryan loved so much they even considered buying a house in Notting Hill during their time there. And Reese loved her character and saw some of herself in Becky. "I definitely related to Becky Sharp. I completely understand what it feels like when you're on the outside of life and you want in so badly that you're willing to do anything to get there. And once you get there, you have to deal with the consequences and tragedies that you've created along the way," Reese explained to the *Record*. She went on to tell *Good Morning America* that "I don't see [Becky Sharp] as bad. I don't see any person as bad. I don't see any character as bad. I think there's something really interesting about the different facets of human nature. And she's a really lonely woman. She's a really lonely little animal. She's, you know, she's a product of how she grew up. No parents and sort of constantly scratching her way to the top."

As filming continued on *Vanity Fair*, it was almost time for a very pregnant Reese to release *Legally Blonde 2: Red, White and Blonde* to theaters. Reese was too pregnant to fly back to the United States to do the required round of press and appearances to promote the movie, so she had MGM, the studio releasing the film, fly the American press overseas to London and come to her instead. Early buzz on the sequel was so strong that there was already talk of a third *Legally Blonde* movie. On opening weekend, *Legally Blonde 2: Red, White and Blonde* raked in nearly $40 million, but still only came in number two at the box office. Elle Woods just couldn't compete against Ah-nold Schwarzenegger and his own sequel, *Terminator 3: Rise of the Machines*. And the reviews for *Legally Blonde 2* were disappointing, though Reese was praised for her flawless portrayal of Elle Woods. The movie ended up grossing $90 million in the United States, but after a few weeks in theaters, the grosses kept plummeting. Sadly, that was the last the world would hear from Elle Woods, as MGM decided to pull the plug on the *Legally Blonde* franchise and halt plans for a third movie due to the less-than-stellar run *Legally Blonde 2* ended up having.

15

Welcome Deacon

Reese was disappointed that *Legally Blonde 2* had not spoken to fans the way she'd hoped or the way that the first movie had. But all was still well in her life. Reese wrapped filming on *Vanity Fair*, a movie that meant a great deal to her personally and professionally, and headed back to Los Angeles with her family in tow so they could prepare for their newest addition.

The announcement that Reese and Ryan were expecting another child took some of the heat off the speculations that their marriage was in trouble—and even if the media was speculating, Reese and Ryan did not let it bother them, because their focus and efforts were solely on their family. "Our life and our family take precedence over our careers and our celebrity," Reese told the *Calgary Sun*. "It's just not important. Ryan and I don't pay attention to what's written about us." And to anyone who thought that any strife their relationship might be facing—even behind closed doors—was due to Ryan's envy of his wife's success, Reese had this to say: "If Ryan was five foot two and blond we might have problems with competition, but it has never been an issue," she told the *Ottawa Sun*.

Reese was still having a hard time grasping that she was a celebrity that the world needed to know more about. She knew that if she had not had the responsibility of her family, that things might have been different and she might have ended up a little less grounded when her star started to rise. "My reality check comes at the end of every day when I go home, make dinner, and play with Ava. Ryan and I don't do the 'glamour couple' thing. We save the clothes and hair and makeup for work," Reese told *W*. "The fun times for us are at home with our daughter and our two dogs. And going to Nashville to see my parents always reminds me that there are lots of other things going on in the world besides movies."

Reese's second pregnancy wasn't exactly planned, but another child was something Ryan really wanted and Reese had always been open to, so when it happened, they were ready and felt blessed. Ava, who was now four years old, was very excited to have a new brother or sister come into her life that she could help take care of and play with, too. "Ryan's really excited about having another baby. And I'm really excited. But Ava's more excited than the both of us. She's dreamy about it," Reese told *People*. "She likes to prepare her room for when her brother or sister comes. I think she'll be a great older sister." And with this pregnancy, Reese was a little bit older (she was now twenty-seven years old compared to being twenty-three when she was pregnant with Ava) and feeling a lot more secure and emotionally prepared. Plus, her life and career were a lot more settled now than they had been the first time around. "On the second baby you don't worry about it as much. The first time, I was, like, panicked. 'I need a crib and I need it by this date!' Now I am much more relaxed," Reese told *People*. "I feel like I'm just finally getting who I am and it's really nice that at the same time, audiences are kind of getting who I am, too.

When I had a kid, it clarified a lot of things to me. I am not a super-cool person. And I've never had the most friends. I'm a mom, and a wife, and that's what I like to be." Reese was also savvier about some of the pitfalls of being pregnant now that she had some experience under her belt. She revealed how she beat her cravings to *People*: "I'm trying not to eat too many potato chips. That's all I want to eat. Potato chips and hamburgers. On the first pregnancy, I gained a lot of weight. I'm trying to be better this time."

Being a mother had also really helped Reese get in touch with her *own* inner child. She'd learned that she really loved the family lifestyle she and Ryan had, so she was looking forward to expanding for that reason, too. "For me having a child is like . . . having a second childhood. I go to all Ava's music classes, and sing louder than all the kids. Like, I'm having such a good time. So I think it sort of brings back those childlike feelings. You know, you still have that energy and those emotions. And it's so great to see. Because you do have that conviction of being a child and that you do know everything. But at the same time, you know so very little. And I see my daughter just throwing herself into things and being so self assured," Reese told *Star Interviews*. "And certainly your whole lifestyle changes. I mean, it's all about what restaurants don't mind having eggs all over the floor. And you know, all the sugar packets thrown at the other customers! But Ryan and I have always been really just normal people who like to eat at Denny's and stuff like that. We love it; we just have such a good time. We had such strong family structures in our lives and in our childhoods that we just have such a great time, raising this perfect little person." Reese and Ryan had a real dynamic going, too, with their responsibilities as parents. Ryan, for example, completely handled potty training Ava and was looking forward to changing diapers again with baby number two. "Ryan's just very instinctual. He knows exactly how to say things or negotiate a temper tantrum."

On October 23, 2003, Reese and Ryan welcomed their son, Deacon Reese, to the world. He was named after Ryan's distant relative Charles Louis "Deacon" Phillippe, who in 1903 pitched and won the first World Series game ever, beating Cy Young, as well as for Hall of Fame football player Deacon Jones.

Life with two children was definitely challenging, but both Reese and Ryan were taking a break from making movies, so they both had plenty of time to stay home and devote themselves to the changes. "You think you are never going to make it through. When they are little babies, you think, I am going to die, I'm so tired, I'm just going to lie down on this carpet, nursing the baby, and I'm just going to die. No one will notice," Reese told *Good Housekeeping*. "But you make it through. Women are so tough." And Reese had plenty of help from proud big sister Ava. "One day as I was changing Deacon's diaper, Ava just started crying. I said, 'What's wrong?' and she wailed, 'You said this was going to be my baby, too, and you're not letting me do any of it! I want to change the diapers! I want to give him the bottle!'" Reese told *Good Housekeeping*. "I was like, 'OK, fine!' They have a really special connection."

Reese and Ryan took pride in making sure that their kids did not become spoiled Hollywood stereotypes because they had celebrity parents and were born into a lot of money. As far as Reese and Ryan were concerned, they had two children who would be treated and brought up like every other child in the rest of the country. "Ryan grew up in Delaware. I grew up in Tennessee, so we don't have a lot of tolerance for children who want their way," Reese told the *Ottawa Sun*. "We're raising our children the way we were raised. They won't get their own credit cards and fancy clothes anytime soon." And with Ava being the oldest, Reese counted on her to be a good influence and role model for Deacon. "I'm really proud of the fact that they aren't spoiled. You know, it's a big deal for Ava that she got two dollars from the tooth fairy. She was so excited that she got to go and pick out a toy for herself for two dollars. But you know what she did? She bought something for her little brother!" Reese recalled to *Good Housekeeping*. "I was so overwhelmed, it wrecked me. She bought him a little toy because she thought it would be good to spend her money on her brother. It's in those small moments that you see who they really are as human beings. It has nothing to do with your personality or your husband's personality. They are just little beautiful, amazing people." And Reese was adamant that unless it was absolutely necessary, she didn't want anyone but her or Ryan raising the children. "We weren't the kind of children that were shadowed. We didn't have nannies. We didn't have housekeepers," Reese told *Interview*. "This whole L.A. culture is so foreign to me, because when I was growing up you wouldn't watch your children every moment. I'm always confused when people bring their children over and then want to sit with them while they play. I think part of the joy of being a child is privacy. Your fantasies and dreams are so important to you at that moment." That's not to say that when the children were with Reese and Ryan there weren't rules to be followed that they were both sticklers about. "Ava can wear all the sparkly stuff she wants, but she's not going to run around with her belly button showing. That's not appropriate," Reese explained to *Good Housekeeping*. "[Ryan] likes them to eat their vegetables, boy. It gets his goat if they don't eat those vegetables. Whooo! You *will* eat your broccoli in our house."

Now that Ava was a little bit older, she was able to understand what her mommy and daddy were doing when they left town or got dressed up in costume on a movie set, though she didn't fully realize that her parents were famous. It was an interesting process for Reese, to watch Ava grasp that concept. "When I was about to start making *Legally Blonde 2*, I was washing my hair in the sink after we had gotten out of the swimming pool. And she said to me, 'Mom, why are you washing your hair?' I said, 'Well, because I have blond hair, and it turns green from the chlorine in the pool.' Then she said, 'Mom, why do you want to be legally blond?' and I said, 'Oh honey, *Legally Blonde* is a movie I did. It's not my hair color,'" Reese told *Marie Claire*. "She said, 'But Mom, why do you want to be *Legally Blonde*, too?' So clearly information is sinking in there somewhere." It was moments like these that really made Reese appreciate what she had with her children and family. "Both of my children are beautiful and healthy and amazing and happy," Reese told *Women's Wear Daily*. "There's just nothing better than spending the day with them. I could just sit around and literally watch them for hours."

Reese found that life with two children in her family meant that her relationship with Ryan—despite what the tabloids were trying to say— was deepening and that they were enjoying their marriage in a more realistic way. "I'm not interested in the fallacy of the Hollywood relationship—'We have perfect children who never cry, we never have problems, we never argue,'" Reese told the *Independent*. "That's just not true. Ryan and I are normal people with normal problems." But Reese went on to tell the *Mail on Sunday* how they managed to stay close and keep things smooth. "We [Ryan and I] do a lot of things for each other. Beyond just taking care of somebody, which is really important, I'll do little special things for him. Like I'll pick up his favorite food or make him his favorite dinner. He likes that. He likes lamb a lot. So I'll cook a really nice lamb chop. He knows my favorite place to get chocolates.

Or he'll buy me music and make me listen to it. He's always doing little things for me. Picking up a movie that I talk about and I know he'd never watch in a million years, he'll buy it for me and he pretends he cares." With two children, they also had new things to worry about— together. "We looked at some fancy things, and Ryan asked, 'What happens if a kid vomits on that?'" And the guy in the store said, 'Kids? Kids aren't allowed in a room with that rug,'" Reese told *W.* "Well, I don't want my kids tiptoeing around our house."

For almost a year, Reese took time just to enjoy her life as a new mom, with no projects to distract her. "The pace gets very hectic in the early success of your career and sometimes it's hard to get off the hamster wheel," Reese told the *Mail on Sunday.* "I feel this time off has been really nice for me, to appreciate what I have. It's so important practicing gratitude for the things that are really important, like my unbelievably beautiful children and my husband and my family."

Vanity Fair hit theaters in September 2004, so Reese did the required rounds of press and magazine photo shoots to promote the movie, but that was it. She had nothing lined up to start filming yet— and neither did Ryan. Then, almost all at once, in late 2004 the two of them were ready to get back into the swing of Hollywood. While they had gone through this before, when Ava was a baby, things were different now that they had two kids to think about when it came to scheduling. Reese was nervous about leaving her kids or not having as much time with them because she truly loved the uninterrupted time she was getting to spend with them. "I love my job, I really do. But there's something about lying on the floor with your kids and hearing them belly-laugh or hearing those deep-down fears they reveal to you when they're in bed and all the lights in the house are out," Reese told *Entertainment Weekly.* "That's really what life's about." Ryan was on the same page, and their family was their priority with no ifs, ands, or buts about it. "Our marriage and our family comes first. It comes before everything else. So before every decision that we make, we talk endlessly. It's always a collective decision," Reese told the *Record*. "It really helps that he understands the business. But in the end, you have to realize, they're all just movies, and you don't want to make a movie at the cost of your relationship."

It did not take long for Reese to line up two projects she would start working on right away, while Ryan was eyeing several movies, including an ensemble film about race relations called *Crash*. Reese signed on to do another romantic comedy called *Just Like Heaven*, as well as a drama based on the life of country singer and legend Johnny Cash. Reese was to play his wife and singing partner, June Carter Cash. It was a role that was going to require much of the research that Reese was famous for when she took on a new character. This time she was playing an actual person, so Reese wanted to live and breathe June Carter Cash; she wanted to see where she lived and where she sang, and meet her living relatives to find out all she could about June. Reese was daunted by the work and time commitment ahead of her and was panicked about how it would affect the kids. "The guilt starts the day the kids are born. If you step away from them for two seconds you immediately feel guilty. My mother will say, in her little southern voice, 'Just get over it. They don't care. As soon as you're gone, they laugh and play like nothing ever happened. They're just trying to manipulate you, Reese!'" Reese told *Good Housekeeping*. "And she's really right. But I have to tell myself that over and over again every time I leave."

It was a good thing that Reese listened to her mother, because the next year of her life was going to change everything for her and Ryan, both together and individually.

16

Heaven on Earth

Before Reese started filming *Walk the Line*, she made the sweet romantic comedy *Just Like Heaven* with actors Mark Ruffalo and Jon Heder, who had just come off the cult hit *Napoleon Dynamite* in which he played the goofy title role. In *Just Like Heaven*, Reese plays Elizabeth, an overachieving doctor so busy she has no time for a social life, who is involved in a horrible car accident that leaves her in a coma no one thinks she will recover from. When her family sublets her apartment to a young widow named David (Ruffalo), Elizabeth suddenly appears and wants David to move out of her apartment. Problem is, she is a ghost, and David is the only one who can see or hear her, except for a psychic named Darryl (played by Heder).

Reese enjoyed making *Just Like Heaven* because she really liked the message about balance and making the most of your life. "This one just had a really nice spiritual message about how important it is to nurture yourself. I think women are natural caretakers. They take care of everybody. They take care of their husbands and their kids and their dogs, and don't spend a lot of time getting back and taking time out. So I like that quality and I like that sort of *Wonderful Life* quality where she gets to see her life for what it was and go back and have another opportunity," Reese told *IGN FilmForce*. "I think that the second-chance element was what really interested me about it and the idea of what happens when you don't nurture your spirit, could it leave you? It's fun to do a comedy and hook people in and then hoodwink them into watching a serious movie. I like to lead in with the comedy and then hit them over the head with a drama." And Reese enjoyed costarring with Mark Ruffalo, as she had admired his other work, including *13 Going on 30* and *You Can Count on Me*. "I think we had a really good time in the movie. We have a very similar sensibility. We're both very family-oriented. We take our work very seriously. I really like the idea that Mark appeals to so many people because he is just who he is. He's not posturing or trying to look pretty or have great hair," Reese told *IGN FilmForce*. "He's just a real man and he's funny. There's a lot of actors nowadays, American actors, that don't think funny is cool, so it's nice to see someone of his caliber doing comedy."

It was odd for Reese, however, to be playing a doctor, tending to patients and wearing scrubs, since medicine was the field her parents had so desperately wanted her to go into if acting didn't pan out. "I love that I am playing a more mature woman, and it was definitely appealing that she's a doctor. It's where I was headed before I got side-tracked into acting," Reese told the *Ottawa Sun*. "On the set, I'd get dressed in my scrubs, take tons of pictures, and send them to my parents, asking if they were finally satisfied."

Secretly, Reese liked living out what could have been if she'd become a doctor and even put in personal requests for the medical jargon in the script to be more complicated. "I kept telling the screenwriter to make the medical words harder. I can say harder words than this," she told the *Mail on Sunday*. "I kept calling my dad, saying, 'Give

me some hard words, Dad." The other part of making the movie that
Reese really got a kick out of was the spiritual and paranormal side of
it. It was a little known fact, but even type A Reese was a believer in
the other side. "I read a lot of books about ghosts and hauntings, but
I've also had personal experiences," Reese told the *Ottawa Sun*. "I was
very close to my grandparents and have seen both of them since they
passed on. Each time it happened it was a comforting experience; it
was definitely not spooky." Twice Reese had paranormal experiences.
"I really believe a certain part of you carries on after you die," she told
the *Record*. "When I was in the hospital, having my children, I felt like
my grandparents were with me. I saw them in the room, and it was
sort of a comforting thing, not spooky at all."

Just Like Heaven was a modest hit, grossing $16 million opening
weekend, and confirmed that Reese was one of the few female stars
who could truly open a movie. But it was received with mixed
reviews and had nowhere near the impact on pop culture that *Legally
Blonde* or *Sweet Home Alabama* had. But her next project, *Walk the Line*,
was going to change her career and standing in Hollywood forever.

17

Reese Walks the Line

Reese felt an instant affinity for June Carter Cash when she accepted the role. June's career, her choices, her relationship with her soul mate, Johnny Cash, and the fact that she was southern all seeped into Reese's soul, and she knew it was her destiny to play this important role. As she told Charlie Rose on his television show: "I felt a real kinship to this character. And I felt a real sense of responsibility to represent her. I had never met her, but I felt a real sense of similarity or character, or some aspect of us, as you know, because I have been working and doing this for a while. I could see what would attract this man [Johnny Cash] who could have any woman he wants to be around, but there was something really genuine about this woman, that she expected him to walk the line, which she says in the movie. And that kind of challenge is rare in someone like that's life. She really challenged him to be a human being with culpability for his behavior and sort of being responsible."

In 2003, right before both Johnny and June Carter Cash passed away within four months of each other, they had each given their blessings for Reese Witherspoon to portray June and Joaquin Phoenix to portray Johnny in a movie about the early years of their career and relationship. As a young girl in Nashville, Tennessee, Reese had looked up to June Carter and Johnny Cash as country music royalty—along with the rest of the state. "Coming from Nashville, I knew a lot about the Carter family, which is sort of the foremost family of country music," Reese told *IGN FilmForce*. "They wrote down a lot of the country songs that were being sung in the backwoods and they put 'em on paper. So June had a long heritage of being the spokesperson for country music and being the face of country music, too."

In the fourth grade, country music was a subject that Reese learned in school, and the Carter family was a majority of her lesson. So when Reese found out that she was being offered the part with June's blessing, she decided she would do everything she could to honor the part and make June and her remaining family members proud. "I understand June Carter and her family. The South is a spiritual place, a place where God is very important in people's lives," Reese told the *New York Times*. "It's about the ritual of family and togetherness and of singing and storytelling. It's about giving back to the community, investing in other people's lives, caring about other people."

June died in May 2003, while Reese was on the set of *Vanity Fair* in London, so unfortunately Reese never had the opportunity to meet her, but she made sure that as soon as she started working on *Walk the Line* she spoke with their children, who were very involved with the film and script to make sure it rang true to the lives of their parents. "When we got on set I called up her children and said, 'I'd really like to meet you and say hi and look you in the eye and tell you I'm going to honor your mother,'" Reese recalled to *Interview*. "So I went down there and got to talk to them and they said that she was really happy about it, too. I guess because she was being played by another southern girl. I was told not to call her children, but I called them anyway, because I just thought if someone were playing my mother I'd want them to look me in the eye and show me who they were."

The children also commented on Reese's physical differences from June. "Well, I was informed upon meeting one of them that my boobs weren't big enough, so I ran immediately to the costume designer and was like, 'I don't think my boobs are big enough!' He said, 'I think we'll be OK.' But as far as accuracy, we were a little off there," Reese told About.com. But Reese also learned a lot about who June Carter Cash was by talking to the children. "They just talked a lot about her personality and how she could just as easily have dinner with the man who pumped gas at the gas station as she could with the queen," Reese recalled to About.com. "She was an amazing sort of person to be so open-minded about humanity."

Talking to June and Johnny's children was just phase one of the research that Reese did to fully embrace the role. It was no surprise that Reese, who had gone undercover in high schools and sororities for past roles, was going to do everything she could to learn what she needed to know about June Carter Cash to properly emulate her. The next thing Reese did was to call her dad and dig back into her own childhood. "My dad cared for a lot of country-music singers and stuff, so he'd tell us things about the country stars. When I first got the job to play June, I called my dad and he helped me out by talking to a lot of his patients who knew her—they knew I was his daughter and I would be playing her, so they were really helpful. Ralph Emery was really helpful. He was this guy who had this early-morning television program, and he'd have the most amazing singers come on and sing at that hour. So he sent me all these wonderful old tapes of June, like back when she was the only girl on an all-male music circuit, singing every romantic, croon-y, jukebox-y song there was. I also went to school with Emmylou Harris's child and Minnie Pearl's grand-daughter. And I went to school with Hannah Crowell, who's Rodney Crowell and Rosanne Cash's daughter. So anecdotally I knew a little bit about what the Cashes' growing-up years must have been like. Like, in kindergarten I remember her talking about her granddaddy and how he saw God. 'He died one day and he came back.' I think in the eighties or later, he had a near-death experience. But June and Johnny were always like the king and queen of Nashville. They're who everybody wanted to know. And Barbara Mandrell—she was big, too. She lived down the street from us. Ray Stevens lived two doors down. Dolly Parton lived down the street from me. Those people were my rock stars."

June's children also opened their home to Reese so she could look at June's things and use them to get a sense of who she was. Reese had already played Maybelle Carter, June's country-singer mother, in a school play when she was younger, so this was an experience she had been building up to since childhood. "June had closets full of furs. I'll never forget it. She just loved fur. Closets full of antique instruments. Mandolins, Autoharps, guitars. Hundreds of them in beautiful condi-tion, properly restored," Reese said to the *Washington Post* of visiting June's home. "So much of the time playing that part I felt her energy. I know that sounds hokey-pokey. She shepherded me through it. I'm not terribly involved in things like ghosts. It really felt like she was there. A feeling of guidance and support. Of overseeing. Things come into your life for a reason. There has to be some kind of destiny to it. I have studied that person and know that family and studied that music. What is the likelihood of all those things aligning? Some of it has to be destiny. That it's fated. Or maybe it's my own idea that I wanted her to condone it. I definitely felt it. When I finished, it was gone."

Reese grasped that June Carter Cash had been misunderstood. Before she and Johnny got together, they both had been married and had other children. For June, that past gave her a reputation— especially because she was out on the road touring. "The movie really didn't scratch the surface of who this woman was. She was living in a world where it was completely unacceptable for her to be doing what she was doing. She lived in the shadow of everyone's judgment. So many people looked at her, thinking, 'That woman slept with so many men and had so many babies by different fathers,'" Reese told *Interview* in an attempt to defend as well as analyze the complexity of June. "I try to think what it was like for a woman to tour around with a bunch of men back then and to have people look at you, like, 'I'm a good Christian, who the hell are you?' How many women are out there touring by themselves with five of the most famous men in country music while maintaining her dignity and sense of self-respect? She did have a wonderful sense of humor and she was tough as nails. You would have to be."

Reese's costar Joaquin Phoenix was equally committed to getting into character and researching his role as the legendary "Man in Black," Johnny Cash. He dressed, spoke, and drank like Johnny—so much so that, after filming on the movie wrapped, he had to check himself into rehab because his drinking habits had intensified so much. But the director of the movie, James Mangold, who had helmed other successful and critically acclaimed movies, such as *Girl, Interrupted*— which won Angelina Jolie an Academy Award—and *Copland* with Robert De Niro, had his own plans for Reese and Joaquin to literally *become* Johnny and June Carter Cash. He insisted that they sing all their own songs and learn to play instruments, just like June and Johnny did. This meant that rehearsals were going to start six months in advance of shooting—a time period during which two movies could normally be completed. Learning to sing was a request that scared both Reese and Joaquin, two methodical and relatively daring actors, so badly that they both panicked—especially Reese. "Every Friday I called my attorney and said, 'Can I please get out of this? What is going to happen if I do?' But ultimately I knew I was going to have to do it. It was really difficult. There were really times when I think they weren't sure if I was going to be able to do it. We rehearsed for six months, and a month into it, it was looking pretty dismal. Because it's one thing to be able to sing in your car and you sound good, or in the shower, to your children. But once you are singing into a mike and they play it back, it takes on a totally different quality. And it took me two different coaches to figure out how to make myself what you want to put into a song," Reese said on the *Charlie Rose Show*. "I don't really know what the motivation was to have Joaquin and I sing. But I don't think some part of it had to do with us learning to be musicians. But the idea that we were going to go through sort of a musical boot camp, where we learned to live that life—it is such a different life than being an actor. Particularly a country musician. There is so much about music that you think, these people are aloof, but in country music it is all about how accessible you are and how open you are and familial you are with your bandmates. They are storytellers."

Reese actually had nothing to worry about, because all of the musical numbers and production were in the hands of the legendary singer, songwriter, and producer T Bone Burnett. He had been nominated for Oscars and Grammys for work he had done on soundtracks

for movies like *Cold Mountain* and *O Brother, Where Art Thou?* Reese
credits Burnett for every song that came out of her during the filming
of the movie. Besides learning to sing, Reese also had to learn to play
the Autoharp—June's instrument of choice. Playing a strange instrument and trying to become as good as June in playing it was even more
traumatizing for Reese than learning to sing. "The singing part was
easier for me than the Autoharp part. Playing the instrument was
really difficult for me. I had never played an instrument. I don't know
how that even happens to people," Reese told About.com. "We found
an Autoharp teacher through Catherine O'Hara who had done it in *A
Mighty Wind*. [O'Hara] basically puts all other actresses who try to
play the Autoharp to shame, and I told her such. It's embarrassing
[that] I have to play Autoharp after her because she's very proficient.
But we found her coach and he ended up coaching Joaquin on guitar,
too. His name is Kit Alderson. He's a great guy."

But even as Reese started to get more into the shoes of a country
singer, she kept having her doubts. "I told Joaquin, 'I'm not going to
do it. Are you going to do it?' He was like, 'If you get out of it, then
I'm getting out of it,'" Reese told the *New York Times*. "You know, we
were both scared and we were sharing our neuroses. Ultimately both
of us knew in our heart of hearts that we had to."

Reese's children became a source of inspiration for her to just
jump in and sing. "My only other singing experience was in summer
camp. They told me how awful I was there and that I should never try
to sing, but just be an actor. I'd really taken that to heart. Jim [Man-
gold] said, 'Just try, and we'll see how it goes from there,'" Reese told
Entertainment Weekly. "And I'm a sucker for 'Just give it a try' because
I'm a mom. I make my kids try everything. We did for four months,
trying to look natural, doing what June and Johnny did for forty years.

Joaquin and I would just go backstage after a scene and shake. 'I'm nervous.' 'No, I'm more nervous.' 'Shut up, I'm nervous.' When you don't have control over your voice, anything can come out. You can really make a fool out of yourself."

Joaquin looked up to Reese and leaned on her during rehearsals. They shared a unique bond, which worked to their advantage on-screen. "Reese was absolutely my pillar throughout the rehearsal process. She was the one who found my guitar teacher, she found our voice coach. I just kind of said, 'Reese, tell me who to call and when to show up and I'll do it,'" Joaquin told *Entertainment Weekly*. "She has real grit and passion and a frankness but there's also this beautiful, warm, maternal quality to her as well. I felt a great confidence in her, which gave me confidence."

Reese was equally moved by Joaquin and his undying commitment to becoming Johnny Cash. "Joaquin helped me immensely. We just supported each other. It was a great journey to go on. He's a really amazing guy. I know how he talks about me supporting him, but his performance alone and the fearlessness he had when he walked onstage inspired everybody," Reese told *Interview*. "The hardest thing was probably having to go, 'Hello. I'm Johnny Cash.' Can you imagine how you would say that? We talked about it the first week, but by the time he got to the day he had to do it, I was just like, 'Wow. He's fearless.' He did it and he did it without twitching and without winking. It was just wonderful." Joaquin's fearlessness still didn't quite put Reese's nerves about singing to rest. Up until the day it was time to start filming performance scenes, Reese's stomach was in knots, and she kept begging James Mangold to hire someone like LeAnn Rimes to take over for her. Reese even had a bucket waiting nearby in case her nerves got the best of her—luckily, she never had to use it.

The scenes in which Reese and Joaquin performed together onstage as June Carter and Johnny Cash were staged exactly as they had really happened, so they had to completely emulate history, and both wanted to make sure that they were dead-on, even if it was odd for them to re-create those moments. "'Time's a Wastin' was the hardest song to sing. It really was hard. We had to have that whole performance with the exchange between them down. The 'You quit that grabbing and clutching on to me now, I'll sing a song.' That was really what happened between June and Johnny," Reese said on the *Charlie Rose Show*. "We have a recording of it. I don't know if it was a live album, but they were talking onstage, and she just kept saying, 'Stop touching me, now get your hands off me. Stop clutching at me.' There are a lot of authentic moments like that, even the proposal at the very end of that song—it really happened. Johnny proposed to her at the end of that performance onstage. They have it on tape." And as filming went on, it got easier and even more familiar for Reese to "channel" June—especially due to some special wardrobe items made available to her. "I wore the exact same outfit June wore in one of her performances," Reese told the *Washington Post*. "It was weird. It fit perfectly."

James Mangold could not have been more impressed or more in awe of both Reese and Joaquin's performances and their transformation into June Carter and Johnny Cash. "Both Joaquin and Reese were so inventive," he said. "If you've got the horses, let them run."

When Reese got the call from James Mangold about playing the part of June Carter Cash, her first instinct was that he had to be mistaken in calling her for such a part. "When Jim Mangold was writing the script, he called me and said, 'Would you like to play June Carter Cash?' I said, 'With all due respect, honey, isn't she like seventy or something? I don't really think I'm ready!'" Reese recalled to the

Record. "Jim said, 'No, no, no, I'm going to do a film about their life when they were young and on tour together.' I couldn't say no to that." James was relieved that Reese agreed, because he knew that there was no one else he could envision in the role. "June was someone who had grown up onstage and evolved into a kind of light comedienne. But in person she was one of the most soulful, honest, and tough women you were likely to meet," he told *Entertainment Weekly*. "In a very similar fashion, Reese's stock-in-trade were these comedic, sassy roles. But she is also a mother and a savvy businesswoman and a very feeling human being who isn't all sass all the time."

From the moment Reese received a copy of the script and began researching June's life and learning to sing, she also received a crash course in everything about the life of this infamous couple and the long road it took for them to finally be together. "They were just people who were deeply in love with each other but couldn't be together because he was married or she was married and they didn't think it was appropriate," Reese told *IGN FilmForce*. "So, you know, it took a long time, but they were finally able to be together." Reese also gained a deeper understand of why they were so revered yet still so tortured by each other. "The thing I respect about the film is, it's a realistic relationship. It's a film where people are tortured because they can't be together," Reese explained to the *Washington Post*. "They're hopelessly flawed and human. That is love and relationships. Life is complicated. Marriage and divorce and children and feelings and social rights and wrongs. It's beautiful in that way." Reese was passionate about accurately portraying and feeling the relationship of June and Johnny in a way that was realistic and would have made them proud. She was in awe of the changes that June made as she grew closer to Johnny, and she wanted to emulate that. "You could see her transformation. She starts out very conservative, in these tight-corseted clothes and tight hairdos in the '50s," Reese told the *Baltimore Sun*. "But when she met John she evolved into a much more sexually liberal woman. It was almost like he freed her."

The experience of becoming June and learning her history taught Reese a lot about women and independence and relationships, which she could apply to her own life. "Cash required a lot of self-possession of June. She had to command respect from talented, famous, popular men surrounded by sycophantic people, often women. She didn't suffer fools, she wasn't interested in unprofessional behavior. And she wasn't interested in a relationship with any of them. Except, from what I've heard, maybe with Elvis," Reese explained to the *Baltimore Sun*. "The struggle women have gone through to be equal in society. It could be suffocating. And here's a woman trying to break out and do things. June's restraint is what defines her in this film. She is so infatuated with this man that she is suppressing her will to be with him at every moment, because of social impropriety and just the difficulty of being with such a large personality who's so troubled. The moment when a woman decides she's going to be with a man is a huge thing — at that time, but even now. It's the moment in which there is no return. And it was important we knew why they capitulated to their infatuation. They had this amazing night of performing onstage— there's video of it, and we watched it, and it was sexually charged."

Reese also thought that June was a woman ahead of her time who didn't let Johnny's fame intimidate or influence her. This was a woman who had Elvis Presley fighting over her, and Reese thought that was just a great part of their story. "Johnny and Elvis had a big fight over June, because Elvis had a crush on her. He was completely infatuated with her and John would just fly into this jealous rage every time his name came up," Reese told the *Toronto Sun*. "The story gives you a lot of hope that it's possible to fall in love at any moment in your life, and you can get it wrong, and you can make mistakes and it might still be there for you. I think they had an amazing connection that was very destined and real and deep-seated."

Reese respected that, even though June was so in love with Johnny, she didn't give in to his advances and pleas to be with her right away. June wasn't impressed that he was a music star as many other women—even famous ones like her—probably would have been. "I think she knew a lot about him. She was a woman who had had a lot of experience before ever meeting him. She had been traveling with her family since she was a child, playing at the Grand Ole Opry and doing stage shows and being on the Louisiana Hayride and singing duets with all sorts of famous men, Elvis Presley and Jerry Lee Lewis," Reese said on the *Charlie Rose Show*. "She really didn't suffer fools. I think moreover than just acknowledging his talent, I think she really saw through all of the glitz and the fame to the real person. I think it's a southern thing. We don't suffer fools down there. We kind of cut through the stuff and get to the real person." Reese also loved the way Johnny truly appreciated June and her talents. "People kept asking me what June got from him. But look at his support of her and his encouragement of her artistry," she told the *Baltimore Sun*. "He recognized the talents she had for writing and performance when a lot of people didn't." James Mangold wasn't surprised that Reese was able to understand June, to identify with her, and analyze her the way that she did. Watching Reese transform into June, he was sure that the reason for it was that they were kindred spirits. "Reese shares more than you know with June. There's another side to Reese. She's incredibly sharp, incredibly well-read. She's a mother of two, a wife, so many things that an actress in her twenties in L.A. is rarely," he told the *Washington Post*. "Each of those choices about her life makes her a vulnerable and feeling and maternal figure. You're struck by what a woman she is. What I mean is that most women of her age are playing girls. And we haven't seen Reese as this woman before in the movies. We've seen her playing, one way or another, a kind of girl. Witherspoon's June will blow people away."

18

Reese's New Man: Oscar

When filming on the movie wrapped, Reese felt a combination of great relief and immense sadness as she let go of the character. She had "become" June Carter Cash for almost a year of preparation and filming. "I love acting, I love the transformation. There are moments where you know everything comes together on a take and that person just becomes the character," Reese said on the *Charlie Rose Show* of how she could feel herself becoming June. "And you become the character and you just feel lost. And those are great moments—those are the moments you work for."

The experience of filming the movie was also grueling, as there were a lot of dark moments and scenes in the film as June tried desperately to save Johnny from his addiction to alcohol and drugs. "It was a very rigorous process. There were a lot of dark days dealing with a lot of difficult things," Reese told the *Mail on Sunday*. "There was a lot of crying [scenes]. Everyday I was [filming scenes] crying and upset and saying, 'Johnny, put the drugs down, I can't take it anymore, Baby!'" Reese also admitted that listening to any Johnny Cash music after the movie wrapped brought up a lot of emotions—and even haunted her just a little. Overall, though, it was a movie that she was extremely proud of, and from which she'd learned a great deal, on many different levels. Plus, her bond with June was one she would never—and could never—forget. "I learned on *Walk the Line* that it's important to scare yourself. To do things you didn't think you were capable of doing. It was really hard for me, this movie. It was hard shaking it off at the end and walking away from it all. There was so much preparation, so much work, and so much commitment. In a way, I wanted to run screaming from it because it was so emotional and I felt such a deep connection to June," Reese told *Interview*. "This sounds southern, but for like a month afterward I really felt like she was with me, and then one day, she left. You read so much about someone and you see so much video of them and talk to so many people about them you start thinking like them. You start to have a lot of their sensibilities, and it really becomes integrated with your own personality. It was hard for me to function in my real life. Plus, I'd just had Deacon, so I was a little vulnerable and emotional."

As promotion started and buzz on the film started to build before it even hit theaters, it suddenly occurred to Reese that people—a lot of people—were actually going to watch her and, even worse, hear her singing. She was terrified that the reviews would be embarrassing, and she did not want real, professional singers whom she respected seeing the movie—especially those in Nashville who were fans and admirers of the real June Carter and Johnny Cash. "I am terrified of people in Nashville seeing it. I ran into people the other day and I just avoided their eyes," Reese confessed to the *Edmonton Journal* before the film hit theaters. "Like, I saw Vince Gill and he's like, 'I can't wait to see the movie.' And I'm like, 'Ugh,' because I'm just scared. And Dolly Parton is like, 'I really want to.' I'm like, 'Please don't see the movie.'"

Ironically, when the movie came out, Reese started getting phone calls from country music labels asking if she wanted to record her own original album of country music! Her answer was always a very polite "No, thank you!" While Reese didn't want to record anything for the public to hear, she wasn't against showing off her new singing talents to those closest to her. For Christmas 2005, Reese created a very special Christmas gift just for Ryan. Ryan's favorite singer is Frank Sinatra, so Reese recorded two of his favorite Sinatra tunes, "I've Got a Crush on You" and "The Best Is Yet to Come," for his ears only.

On November 18, 2005, *Walk the Line* hit theaters. Reese didn't have to worry about her singing in the movie being panned, because when the reviews came out, no one had anything bad to say about her singing—or her performance. Even so, the release of the film to theaters was bittersweet for Reese. The world was about to see what she had poured her heart and soul into and worked on for so long. "With this film, I learned a lot and challenged myself and did things I didn't think I was capable of doing and stuck it out and it was a good thing. And now it's done," Reese reflected to *Interview*. "It's always sad when a movie comes out because it's not yours anymore. It belongs to the world. It's like your little secret is out."

It was a secret, however, that the world was lucky to be let in on, as the reviews were glowing. The word in the industry was that both Reese and Joaquin were shoo-ins to take home Academy Awards. John Carter Cash, the son of June and Johnny, was blown away by Reese's portrayal of his mother. "Reese took on the role with a full heart," he told the *Washington Post*. "She played it with reverence and style and I know my mother would have loved it."

As awards season kicked off, Reese started taking home awards for *Walk the Line*, ranging from almost every major city's critics' circle award to the prestigious National Society of Film Critics award. Then Reese won a Golden Globe. This was the first major award that indicated she would likely be nominated for an Academy Award.

With all the attention and buzz surrounding Reese, Joaquin, and the film, the night of the Golden Globes actually helped them relax and focus on something other than the upcoming Oscar nominations. Reese and Ryan sat at the same table as Joaquin, where they laughed, cheered, and were one of the rowdiest groups of the night.

Ryan was sure that both Reese and Joaquin would walk away with awards that night—but Joaquin was not so sure. In fact, Ryan was so sure that he would not lose—and Joaquin was so sure that he would— that they bet all the money in Ryan's wallet (a whopping $220) that Joaquin's name would be called to the podium. That night, Ryan could not have been happier to have his wallet cleaned out as Joaquin and Reese won Golden Globes for Best Actress and Actor in a Musical or Comedy. The day after the awards, however, no one cared that Reese had won "only" a Golden Globe. The focus instead was on the fact that Reese had worn the same Chanel dress that Kirsten Dunst had worn to the Golden Globes in 2003! Soon afterward, the focus was back on the awards and accolades Reese was being showered with when her industry peers awarded her with a Screen Actors Guild Award, another prestigious honor that is often a sign that Oscar gold is around the corner.

On the morning that the Oscar nominations were announced, Reese and Joaquin discovered that they had both been nominated for the top prize. But the morning was extra special for Reese, because a movie called *Crash* that Ryan had a part in was nominated for Best Picture. It was truly an amazing morning for the couple—both of their careers were riding high at the same time once again. Reese, however, wasn't even in the same country as Ryan when the news broke! "I was in Berlin at the time, asleep on a couch because I was jet-lagged. My publicist came in screaming, and I thought it was my daughter and I was dreaming," Reese recalled to the *Toronto Sun*. "But they woke me up and I was very excited. I called my husband and my mother right away, which made it even more exciting, because *Crash* was nominated, too." Reese's competition in the category was an eclectic group of experienced actresses. They were Judi Dench in *Mrs. Henderson Presents*, Felicity Huffman in *Transamerica*, Keira Knightley in *Pride and Prejudice*, and Charlize Theron in *North Country*. It was a tough race, but in all the pre-Oscar commentary, Reese kept being mentioned as the front-runner. She was trying to take the pressure off winning as best she could. "I think every actor there wants to win, otherwise what is the point? But listen, I am twenty-nine years old. I'm really lucky to be there, and whatever happens, I've been blessed really already. I have plenty of awards for this movie, and if this was it for me I'd be really content," she told the *Toronto Sun*. "[I keep them] in various places. My daughter Ava sneaks them off to her room and dresses them up and colors them. She's become quite jaded about the whole awards thing. Every night, Ryan and I come home, she's like, 'Well did you get it or not. Where is it? Are you going to take it to my room?' It's sweet, actually; she enjoys it."

On March 5, 2006, Reese and Ryan arrived hand in hand at the Kodak Theater at Hollywood and Highland in Los Angeles, where they walked the red carpet of the Seventy-eighth Annual Academy Awards. Reese was positively beaming with pride as she spoke to reporters and posed for photographers. She had Ryan by her side, and her parents were there, as well, to show their support (and finally accept the fact that Reese was definitely not ever going to become a doctor). Once inside the auditorium, all she had to do was sit back and relax. It was going to be a long while until the Best Actress award was presented! When Jamie Foxx, the previous year's recipient of the Best Actor Oscar, walked out onstage, Reese knew the time had come. She gave a big smile and cuddled up next to Ryan as the camera showed her on the screen. And then Jamie opened the envelope. "And the Oscar goes to . . ." Jamie said as Reese's heart dropped into her stomach. *"Reese Witherspoon."*

Reese ran up to the stage and gave what has now become one of the most emotional and inspiring Oscar acceptance speeches to date. As she walked up to the podium, she clutched the award she'd worked so hard to achieve, and then she said these moving words:

"Oh, my goodness. I never thought I'd be here my whole life, growing up in Tennessee. I want to say Johnny Cash and June Carter had a wonderful tradition of honoring other artists and musicians and singers, and I really feel that tradition tonight. It is very important, and I really feel it. So I want to thank the academy for this incredible honor. I want to say thank you to so many people who helped me create this role. Everyone at Fox, Cathy Konrad, James Keach, for producing the film. A very special thank-you to Jim Mangold, who directed the film and also wrote this character. Who is a real woman. Who has dignity and honor, and fear, and courage, and she's a real woman. And I really appreciate that. It was an incredible gift that you gave me. So thank you. And T Bone Burnett for helping me realize my lifelong dream of being a country music singer. Thank you, T Bone. And I want to say thank you to Joaquin Phoenix, who just put his heart and soul into this performance. His commitment and passion for this character and for this performance was just remarkable, and I feel so lucky to have gone on this journey with you. I am so blessed to have my family here tonight. My mother and my father are here. And I just want to say thank you so much for everything, for being so proud of me. It didn't matter if I was making my bed or making a movie. They never hesitated to say how proud they were of me. And that means so very much to a child. So thank you, Mom and Dad. I want to say thank you to my wonderful husband and my two children (who should be going to bed!). And thank you for loving me so much and supporting me. And I want to say that my grandmother was one of the biggest inspirations in my life. She taught me how to be a real woman, to have strength and self-respect, and to never give those things away. And those are a lot of qualities I saw in June Carter. People used to ask June how she was doing, and she used to say, 'I'm just trying to matter.' And I know what she means. You know, I'm just trying to matter, and live a good life and make work that means something to somebody. And you have all made me feel that I might have accomplished that tonight. So thank you so much for this honor."

Ryan watched from his seat with tears in his eyes as his wife accepted the biggest honor of her career. Just a little while later, Ryan's movie *Crash* won Best Picture, to complete one of the most special, memorable, and meaningful nights they had had together as a couple in a very long time. Unfortunately, it was probably one of their last.

19

"Kaput" Goes the Marriage

After the Oscars, Reese took some much needed time off to rejuvenate, spend time with her family, and get herself out of the public eye. Ryan, however, was the busiest he had been in a long time: he was in the process of filming two movies back-to-back. The first was the true story of the greatest security breach in U.S. history in a film called, what else? *Breach*, and the second was a film about soldiers in Iraq called *Stop Loss*.

Reese had no films in the works and was happy to have the much needed and much deserved time for herself. The only drama was wrapping up a lawsuit with a paparazzo named Todd Wallace who was arrested after he pushed a friend of Reese's and struck her friend's daughter while they were at Disney's California Adventure Park for Ava's birthday celebration. The pushing happened as a result of Wallace aggressively trying to get shots of Reese and her children. Reese was not going to let this incident slide. She did not want her children to be unable to enjoy the little things in life, like having uninterrupted fun time at a theme park! Ironically, Wallace was found dead in his apartment in Los Angeles shortly before the case was set to go to trial. Many speculated that he had committed suicide to avoid the possible punishment, since it was now a law in California that paparazzi who assaulted celebrities in the course of trying to photograph them would be slapped with triple damages.

But despite being out of the limelight for the most part, things didn't stay quiet for long. Rumors started to surface that Reese and Ryan were once again having marital troubles. There were stories that at the after-parties on Oscar night, they had each gone their separate ways and barely acknowledged the other's existence. Onlookers described each of them as looking unhappy.

Just a few weeks after the Oscars, on March 22, Reese's thirtieth birthday, when she had to beg Ryan to spend that special day with her, she started to panic that maybe their relationship had hit a wall. The tabloids got wind of the fact that Reese and Ryan often had fights because Reese didn't think Ryan spent enough time with her. And the only way they managed to be together on her birthday was that their personal trainer came to the house and they worked out as a pair. To have such negative and harmful stories floating around was devastating to Reese. She was set on creating a public facade that everything, from her career to her marriage to her children, was perfect.

In the summer of 2006, Reese sued a tabloid after they falsely reported that she was pregnant with her third child and was hiding it from the producers of her latest movie. Through the years, Reese had been so defensive that her marriage was solid that she had several times threatened other magazines with lawsuits if they were going to print otherwise.

But for most of 2006, Ryan was away from Reese while he filmed movies. The rumors that he was unfaithful and unhappy just would not die. While he was in Toronto filming *Breach* (a full month before the reports of their iciness to each other after the Oscars) the tabloids reported that Ryan had invited a hostess from a club where he had been partying back to his hotel room. This was a long way from the romantic gentleman Reese had exchanged love letters with after a single meeting. The rumblings that Ryan could not get past the fact that Reese's star had risen dramatically past his own would not go away, either. Apparently Ryan had trailed behind Reese as they entered a hot pre-Oscar party. When a security guard asked Ryan for his pass to enter, he became furious and snapped, "My wife *is* my pass!" And, unable to accept the fact that Reese was on the verge of winning an Oscar, Ryan started arrogantly telling people that the next year (2007) he would be up at the podium getting his turn to shine as the Best Actor winner for his role in the Clint Eastwood–directed World War II drama *Flags of Our Fathers*. Sadly, Ryan's prediction was wrong, as he was not even nominated, and the film received lukewarm reviews at best.

Fast forward to October 16, 2006, at the New York City premiere of *Flags of Our Fathers*. Reese and Ryan attended together, but everyone in attendance noticed that all was not well between them. As they got out of their limo, neither one looked happy; in fact, they looked downright miserable.

Later on that night they went to the after-party together, but both immediately went their separate ways. Reese is rarely seen drinking in public, but that night it was obvious that she was a little inebriated. She probably needed the buzz to take some of the edge off of the tension between her and Ryan. They started out blatantly ignoring each other, but before long Reese ran into her husband and suddenly they were arguing so loud everyone at the party could hear—though people tried to avert their eyes and ears. Reese called Ryan an "asshole," and he told her to stop because she was embarrassing him. "Oh, I embarrass you, Ryan? How do I embarrass you?" Reese seethed at him before storming off to the bathroom. Throughout their relationship, Reese had never been quite as into partying and going out as Ryan was. She rarely joined him for nights out at clubs, and when she did, it was usually reported that she looked uncomfortable (especially since so many girls didn't hesitate to flirt with Ryan, even knowing that his wife was right there) and wanted to leave before he was ready. But never had they fought so publicly—and confirmed to the world that perhaps all the speculation that their marriage was rocky was based on truth. So, two weeks later, on October 30, 2006, it was not exactly a shock when Reese and Ryan released a joint statement to the press via their publicists that they were formally separating as a couple. The statement read: "We are saddened to announce that Reese and Ryan have decided to formally separate. They remain committed to their family and we ask that you please respect the privacy and the safety of their children at this time."

Fighting was not an uncommon occurrence for Reese and Ryan, but it had always before been done in private. Reports started surfacing that some of their brawls had been so bad that Ryan would leave home for several days and go sleep in his office in Venice. And their fights were usually about mundane things, like how they should renovate their house or why they couldn't train their dogs properly. But as soon as their separation was announced, nothing was private anymore. There was more embarrassment and shame for Reese to live out in public to come. From August until right before the *Flags of Our Fathers* premiere in October, Ryan had been filming his movie *Stop Loss* around the globe, from Morocco to Austin, Texas. Reese had come to visit Ryan in Austin, but for the most part they did not see each other while he was filming. It was probably for the best, as Ryan was getting quite cozy with his Australian costar, Abbie Cornish. The press called their time together a "fling," but according to published reports, it was a little more involved than that, and when Reese found out, it pushed her over the edge. She could no longer deny what was so obvious— her marriage was over. Reese had confided to her girlfriends through the years that she was suspicious of Ryan's wandering eye. But she never could bring herself to admit it was true—she was in love with Ryan and always defended him. He was the father of her children, and she couldn't get enough of the way he was with them. Every time Reese watched Ryan with the kids, even with doubts of his faithfulness in her head, she fell in love with him all over again. But as more and more evidence emerged that Ryan had a full-fledged relationship with Cornish, Reese couldn't live in denial anymore. It was over.

For a married man, Ryan was not exactly discreet about the time he was spending with Cornish in Austin. While dining at a local sushi restaurant called Kenichi, they were seen openly making out, with her legs on top of Ryan's under the table. Ryan had rented a loft apartment, and Cornish was seen spending a lot of time there—sometimes even entire days at a time. Some eyewitnesses told the tabloids that she would often leave in the morning looking as if she had just rolled out of bed. Ryan even tipped the hostesses at several of the restaurants they dined at together so they could have a more private area to sit in. While out at clubs, they would snuggle with each other and act very affectionate. Ryan was also spotted without his wedding ring throughout almost the entire time he was in Austin. On the set, too, they were open about their affair. It was shocking for the rest of the cast that Ryan, a married man, would be so open about cheating. It was almost as if he was trying to get caught. And reports had started

surfacing that Ryan had been confiding to anyone who would listen—
friends, costars, even strangers he struck up conversations with—that
he was not happy at home and that he wanted his marriage to end.

The whole thing could have very well happened as a result of a
casting director with an eye for chemistry. Avy Kaufman, the casting
director for *Stop Loss*, had also cast Michelle Williams and Heath
Ledger in *Brokeback Mountain* and, well, they met for the first time
while making the movie, fell in love on the set, and had a baby
together. Reese tried hard not to believe the rumors that her husband
had so openly cheated on her until he returned home and she got hold
of his BlackBerry. Looking through it, she found tons of e-mails
between Cornish and Ryan that confirmed that they were definitely
more than just costars and absolutely more than just friends.

Reese was devastated and, more than anything, she was furious.
For years she had quieted the suspicions in her head and given Ryan
the benefit of the doubt. She truly loved him and could not believe he
not only didn't love her in return but would betray her in this way.
But this time was different. She couldn't let it go anymore, and she had
to face reality and accept what was happening. Reese confronted Ryan
in an emotional scene. He didn't even try to deny it, as he had done so
many times in the past. According to reports, Ryan came clean that he
had indeed had an affair with Cornish. It was a turning point for
Reese. She couldn't sweep this under the rug and put on a happy face
as she had done in the past.

The fact of the matter was that 2006 was Reese's year. She had won
an Oscar and shortly afterward become the highest-paid actress in
Hollywood, making $29 million for a movie she signed on to called
Our Family Trouble. Reese's salary surpassed even that of Julia Roberts,
the reigning queen of highest-paid actresses. Julia's highest had been

$24 million for *Mona Lisa Smile*. Reese was basking in the success her hard work had delivered and in her status as America's sweetheart. With her public image as sweet and adorable, the news that Ryan had reportedly cheated on her instantly made the public feel sympathy for her and reproach for Ryan. Reese refused to talk to the press, but Ryan had to do some damage control for his reputation. He told *People* shortly after the separation was announced, "I'm not a perfect person, but I'm not guilty of a lot of the things I have been accused of. My priority is and always has been the health and safety of my family."

Just a few days later, Reese officially filed for divorce. Filed through the Los Angeles Superior Court, the details of the court papers revealed that Reese had asked for joint custody of the children and Reese sought physical custody of her kids and that Ryan be granted visitation rights. Reese also requested that the court not grant spousal support for Ryan.

The news that Reese and Ryan were officially ending their marriage was shocking news to both of their families. Ryan's mom, Susan Phillippe, told *People*, "Our hearts are broken and our family is in mourning. We are heartbroken and worried—about the children and everything. This is devastating. We just hope things can work out." Reese would not speak to the press and instead was happy to bury herself back in her work as she headed to the set of *Rendition*, her first movie since *Walk the Line*.

In the movie, in which Reese costars with Jake Gyllenhaal, Reese plays the pregnant wife of a terrorism suspect who searches for the truth behind her husband's disappearance. Lucky for her, the filming was going to take her around the globe, to places like Morocco, South Africa, Washington, D.C., and, of course, home to Los Angeles. The first scenes were filmed in L.A., and Reese decided to request that no cell phones be allowed on set. She didn't want any members of the cast or crew taking photos with cell phone cameras of her with her costar. The last thing Reese wanted was for anyone to think that she had moved on to a postdivorce fling with Gyllenhaal. What Reese did want was for her children to be happy and not scarred by the repercussions of the divorce. As much as she had been hurt by Ryan, she couldn't deny that he was an amazing father, and she did not want her kids to grow up without a strong father figure in their lives. Photos soon surfaced of Ryan taking the kids out for afternoons in the park or to lunch at McDonald's. Reese revealed a bit more of what this time in her life was like to *Harper's Bazaar* in April of 2007, saying, "I'm just sort of living day by day. You can have ideas of what you think things are going to be and what your life is going to be, and sometimes it changes. You can't plan everything. Life just tells you that the universe constantly reminds you that you're not in control. You're not in charge of the whole world—what a revelation!"

In February 2007, Ryan came out of hiding to start promoting *Breach*, and he spoke out about what he was going through. His main concern, as he told *Extra*, was Ava and Deacon. "It's unfortunate when you have kids, but I signed up for this and have to deal with it," Ryan said. "I don't read the magazines or watch the shows. It's hard when people follow me to my kid's school."

But on the *Ellen DeGeneres Show*, Ryan revealed more specifically how his family was coping with the divorce and whom he was leaning on for support. It was the first time any indication was given as to what was going on with Reese and Ryan, as Reese was set on maintaining her privacy after the mortifying details of Ryan's infidelity were made so very public. "This is the most devastating time in my life," Ryan told DeGeneres. "Going through something like this, as difficult as it is, my daughter has been the inspiration—my seven-year-old daughter, Ava, is beyond her years in conscientiousness and maturity. I know it sounds pathetic. I'm a thirty-two-year-old guy, but my seven-year-old daughter is getting me through the toughest time in my life, and that's beautiful, too." Ryan went on to tell everyone that Deacon was holding up, as well. "He's all right, you know. I mean, three-year-olds. He's fun, every day he says something that makes me laugh, warms my heart. They're hanging in there. It ain't easy. It's devastating, but the bottom line is the focus on the children, and they're doing amazingly well and that's really all that matters."

Reese, however, kept her head high and stayed out of the spotlight for the next few months while she filmed *Rendition*. When she arrived at the 2007 Academy Awards to present the Best Actor award, she was positively beaming in a silk jacquard gown custom-made for her by Olivier Theyskens for Nina Ricci complete with an eighty-three-carat diamond Van Cleef & Arpels cuff. Reese made every Best Dressed list after the ceremony, and the talk of the town was how she was clearly trying to tell Ryan to "eat his heart out" now that he could no longer have her. Not to mention that it was widely reported that Reese wanted to knock everyone's socks off with her look that night because she was finally ready to start dating again and figured there was no better way to send out that message than nailing her look at the Oscars.

Reese also had the help of her girlfriends to get her through—like actress Selma Blair, with whom she was still friends so many years after costarring in *Cruel Intentions* and *Legally Blonde* together. Selma had gone through a divorce, too, so she was happy to be there for Reese as she understood her pain.

"[Reese] was always there for me. There was one day when I was pretty blue and she came over to my house trying to get me out of my morning frock," Selma recalled to *Harper's Bazaar*. "She's the kind of woman who will come over and look through your closet and help pick out clothes, do your makeup—that kind of thing."

But, in April 2007, Reese found herself back on the cover of all the tabloids with some big news. She was dating her *Rendition* costar Jake Gyllenhaal. Reese and Jake reconnected during reshoots for the movie, and they could not suppress their mutual crushes on each other any longer. For almost two months before the tabloids caught wind of their budding romance, they "tried out their courtship," as a friend of Reese's told *Us Weekly*. Jake's last high-profile relationship, which had been with actress Kirsten Dunst, had reportedly ended because Jake was a homebody and Kirsten was a party animal. Reese never was a fan of Ryan's desire to go out to the clubs, so right off, Jake and Reese were on the same page. Plus, Jake came from his own close-knit family and loved how devoted Reese was to her own children. Jake told *Us Weekly*, "I'm at a period in my life when I'm figuring out my idea of who I am and what I want and how to hold onto love—all that big stuff."

Reese insisted that things with Jake move slowly, as she was still reeling from the pain of her divorce. It didn't help that Ryan was constantly in the tabloids with reports of hitting on all of young Hollywood—including Lindsay Lohan. Jake, too, wanted to be sure of where things were heading, as he and Ryan were workout buddies at their gym. Ever the gentleman, he did not want to make waves.

But overall, Reese was hoping her new romance would work out. She was at the top of her game—slimming down from a size six to a size two post-divorce—and in the spring of 2007 she was ready to allow herself to be happy again. "I look forward to my work. I love my children," Reese told *Harper's Bazaar*. "At this time in my life, it's about spending time with my kids, really connecting with my friends. I'm very lucky. I have a really great life."

20
Reese vs. Hollywood

Reese has come a long way from the early days of her career, when people would chase her down the street in their car and get into accidents trying to get a few words with her. The only problem was that, back then, the crazed fans were more disappointed than ecstatic when they finally came face-to-face with Reese—because they actually thought they were chasing Alicia Silverstone! "A man got his car smashed because he thought I was her," Reese told *Marie Claire*. "I was like, 'I'm so sorry you smashed your car this way.' He was like, 'Oh, man, I can't believe I stopped my car for *you*.'"

Today, Reese definitely doesn't have to worry about fans mistaking her for anyone else, as she is one of the most recognizable faces in the world. Instead, she has to worry about the paparazzi—and keeping them away as they flock to her in an attempt to get a shot with her and her kids or whoever her post-Ryan boyfriend will be. It's a side of fame that Reese does not have any patience or tolerance for. "I had an incident where the paparazzi ran me off the road and hit my car. They subsequently paid for it. I absolutely believe in the First Amendment, and that they have a right to take pictures of public figures, but

illegal behavior is not acceptable," Reese told the *Chicago Sun-Times*.
"I've seen some changes lately. I've seen a little more respect from
these photographers. I hope I made an impact on this issue. It's not
OK to do illegal things and get away with it."

Reese has never understood the motives of the paparazzi to follow
celebrities, as she told *Glamour UK* shortly after *Legally Blonde* was
released and the interest in Reese quadrupled. "The paparazzi follow
behind you in dark vehicles with tinted windows so you can't see who
they are. Then they follow you inside, wait behind a door, and jump
out at you to make you react. It's insane. I just can't figure out what
the big hullabaloo is about seeing someone go to Starbucks. Here's the
news flash: people who are in the public eye . . . drink coffee." Just a
few years later, Reese was just as baffled by the interest—especially in
the most mundane of activities—that the paparazzi had in celebrities,
but she was attempting to put a more positive spin on it, as she told
the *National Post*. "I can't believe anyone cares about all the pictures of
me at the grocery store or at the preschool. I mean, it's like, every day
I am wearing the same sweat suit. It's like, 'Is this really interesting?'
But if pictures of me looking like that make people feel like, 'Hey, she's
a slob like me,' I'm all for it. Because I am—I am a slob."

"Slob" is definitely not what comes to mind when Hollywood talks
about Reese. As one of the most sought-after stars in the world, Reese
has created her star power by knowing how to play up her strengths
and always leaving her troubles at home. You'd never know she was
going through a divorce or dealing with any sort of trouble in her life
when you watch Reese walk a red carpet or attend a big Hollywood
event. That behavior is greatly attributed to the "southern" character,
and at times it worried some of Reese's friends. Some were worried
that perhaps she was being a little *too* OK with the way things

unraveled, and not allowing her true emotions to come out even as just a release in private or among close and trusted friends.

Regardless of how Reese handles the things going on in her private life, her public persona is what sets her apart. "Once you get to a place where you've had films that have done well, you get scared that the next ones won't do as well. People are always telling me it's OK if you fail, but that's hard. Actors are all basically replaceable," Reese told *Entertainment Weekly*. "You can have a series of not-so-great movies and everybody's off you and you have to be happy that you had your moments. I'd like my life to be a string of moments, good and bad."

Reese's abilities to stay composed in the spotlight, to never let anyone see her sweat; to choose quality movie roles; and to remain honest and open in interviews are just a few of the many things that have made her stand out among her peers in young Hollywood. "I'm not the next Julia [Roberts] or the next Meg [Ryan]," Reese told *Marie Claire*. "I'm just me and they are who they are. I think there is room for everybody." Those who have worked with Reese agree, including Mark Waters, who directed her in *Just Like Heaven*. "It's not like Reese Witherspoon is Daniel Day-Lewis, like, 'Oh, look, she's the guy with Down syndrome in this part and she's walking with a limp and a beard in this one.' That thing that you find captivating and charming about her on screen are the things that are captivating and charming about her in real life," Waters told *Entertainment Weekly*. "But the defining characteristic of Reese is someone who is really intelligent. She really doesn't suffer fools, which can be a problem when she is working with fools." Reese prides herself on not suppressing who she is just to appease directors and other strong personalities in Hollywood. Some might be chastised for speaking up, but Reese has earned respect for her fearless approach. "I get torn apart all the time for having a personality. But I got thrown into the fire early, and I feel very clear about things, even if I hate myself for being too revealing or opinionated. I don't like people who talk in circles about nothing," Reese explained to *Entertainment Weekly*. "People who give you the runaround because they don't want to answer a question or they just want to manipulate you by not giving you enough information. Just say it: 'Will you wear the bikini?' 'No.' Now we're done."

"I don't know why everyone finds my life so interesting," Reese told *Women's Wear Daily*. "I am just kind of a dork." Seeing herself as a "dork," or just a regular girl from Nashville, is what Reese has built her career on and what has made her female fans able to relate to her. There are no illusions to make the world think she was born famous, glamorous, and full of confidence. "I've learned that being in the public eye, it's how you feel about yourself," Reese explained to *Teen*. "If I was concerned with everything I read or saw on myself, it would eat me up and I'd think, 'Oh! I can't go outside!' I know what is true about me. Other people's opinions of you don't matter." Reese worked hard and had a talent and used that talent—and only that talent—to get ahead, instead of relying on things like acting "dumb" or showing off her body. It's something she takes a lot of pride in. "Funny doesn't sag. Yeah, you can be sexy all you want, but you know, I have never wanted my talent to be based on how I look or how I look in this year's clothes or anything like that," Reese said on *Good Morning America*. "I mean, I always felt that being funny is what made me have friends and got me where I am today. It is always so important to have a sense of humor about life. People appreciate that so much."

Watching other young actresses take the opposite approach has always confused Reese, and she has spoken openly about it in the hope of reaching out to them. "What gets me is how many women, young women, give up their power and sense of self thinking they are going to get more out of life if they take off their clothes and objectify themselves, instead of functioning on the principle that they are smart and capable, that you can be an actress and not be on the covers of T-and-A magazines," Reese told *Marie Claire*. "I'm flabbergasted by how many legitimate actresses do that. It blows my mind." Reese went on to tell *Flaunt*, "I'm always befuddled by young women who have great opportunities, then put themselves in a mediocre movie. Why are they betraying themselves? Why would anyone do that? I really am concerned for other people and why they destroy themselves and why they don't value themselves enough to make a good decision."

Fame is a delicate subject for Reese, because while she certainly knew that being on the covers of magazines and being hounded by the paparazzi was a sign that she was famous and therefore succeeding in her career, it was never the thing she'd set out to be an actress for. She became an actress because she loves to act.

Reese told *Good Housekeeping*, "Sometimes I feel like a dinosaur. The other day I read something about myself that said I liked collecting embroidery and antique lace, and I thought, 'Oh man, I sound like my grandma!'" But Reese's old-school sensibility comes from her southern upbringing, which is an inherent part of what she stands for in her personal and public lives. "I grew up in Tennessee. We didn't know what Louis Vuitton was. I think that is a good thing. I had to order all my prom outfits out of catalogs," Reese told *W*. "It's a different sensibility. I had manners classes when I was eight years old. One day recently, I was driving with my mother and got stopped for a speeding ticket. I said, 'I'm so sorry, officer.' And the officer said to my mother, 'Ma'am, I've met a lot of movie stars, but your daughter has excellent manners.'" But Reese isn't always so prim, proper, and utterly serious. She recognizes that deep down that's an impossible task, even for an Academy Award–winning actress who's built a career on those characteristics! "You know what? Getting older, I think you have to accept that we are all big goobers. I think that is what brings you peace in life: realizing sooner, rather than later, that we are all big goobs!" Reese told *W*. "It is just a waste of time trying to be or act together—because nobody is together."

21

What's Next?

With her enormous power as a leading actress and movie producer, Reese could very well add "director" to her résumé in the near future and become the ultimate triple threat. "I would love to [direct]. I think it's just a matter of time. I think it's hard when I have little kids to look after now, so I don't have the time to concentrate," Reese told *IGN FilmForce*. "It'd be hard to focus, but probably when I get older I would really love to write more and probably direct. Maybe, maybe. I go back and forth. It seems like a lot of work."

For now, Reese is keeping her attention on acting and sticking to her rule of making only one film a year so she can spend time with her children, which is more necessary than ever now that she is divorced and the time she spends with them is on her own. She is also very particular about what roles she chooses and refuses to make anything just for the sake of making it. "It's actually easier for me to say no than it is to say yes! Because I know when I go into something that I am going to put my heart and soul into it, and that takes a lot of effort," Reese told *Star Interviews*. "You have to really love something to say, 'OK, every day of this, I'm going to love this project, and love this character.'

I'm very particular about the roles I choose because I want to be in movies that I would like to see. And we all have our own ideas of what we like to see. So I just try to be very choosy."

There is more to Reese's process than just loving the project—she has to feel it, too. "I have a weird process, but the main thing is like this: I hear [the character's] voice in my head," Reese told *Mr. Showbiz.* "There are a lot of wonderful scripts my agents can't believe I pass on, but I do because I can't hear the voice. It doesn't appeal to me then, I'm really careful. Unless I hear the voice, I can't do it." And when Reese can hear that voice and absolutely loves a project, that's when the Oscar-winning magic happens. "I consider myself a character actor," Reese explained to *InStyle.* "I love losing myself, losing my voice, finding someone else's physicality. That's my passion."

Reese wrapped filming on *Rendition* in the summer of 2007 and released the fairy-tale-esque film *Penelope* then, too. *Penelope,* produced by Type A Productions, starred Christina Ricci in the title role as a girl cursed with a pig's face. Since Reese worked hard behind the scenes as a producer on the film, she took only a small part, as Penelope's best friend, Annie. *"Penelope* is a modern-day fable with an incredible production design and a dark sense of humor," Reese told *USA Weekend.* "It has an uplifting message and a great story about learning to appreciate who you are." Christina loved having Reese as her boss—and friend. On set, Christina was impressed by how "smart, eloquent, and thoughtful Reese was. She doesn't create any tension or competitive feelings," she told *Harper's Bazaar.* "You feel she's genuine in her desire to see other women experiencing success. She was so much more mature than me—and she still is. I always felt like a bit of a goofball around her."

Set for release in 2008 is the romantic comedy *Sammy,* which

Type A Productions is producing, as well. It was directed by Lasse Hall-ström, who was nominated for an Academy Award in 2000 for directing the quirky drama *The Cider House Rules*. In *Sammy*, Reese plays a modern-day Dr. Doolittle who has the special ability to communicate with animals. She meets and falls in love with a guy who can give her a run for her money because he can communicate with the dead.

Reese has gone from being a hard-headed young actress to being one of the most polished, admired, and celebrated stars in the world. She has that rare ability to make men fall in love with her and women want to spend the day shopping with her. Despite the hardships going on in her life, she wants only what is best for her family and herself. She's a rare celebrity, the kind who comes along only once every generation. How does she do it? We'll let her complete this story by telling you herself. "I just feel lucky to work. I feel like I am in such a rare position that I have gotten to get this far in this business as a woman *and* that I still am presented with challenging roles with great writers and great directors and great costars. These roles come along so infrequently. Maybe every five years you get to see a role that really you are never going to read anything like it again ever in your life. So you just have to keep looking for that and hoping it comes your way. You've got one role and twenty-five actresses that want it, you know?" Reese told About.com. "I stay grounded because basically I know my grandmother would be mortified if I did anything less. I grew up with a lot of emphasis on how to carry yourself. You just kind of are who you are in life, don't you think?"

Filmography and Television Appearances

FILMOGRAPHY

1991

The Man in the Moon

Reese Witherspoon (Danielle "Dani" Trant), Sam Waterston, Tess
Harper, Jason London

MGM/Pathé Entertainment

Producer: Mark Rydell

Director: Robert Mulligan

Screenplay: Jenny Wingfield. Cinematography by Freddie Francis.
99 minutes

1993

A Far Off Place

Reese Witherspoon (Nonnie Parker), Ethan Embry, Jack Thompson,
Sarel Bok

Amblin Entertainment/Walt Disney Pictures

Producers: Eva Monley and Elaine Sperber

Director: Mikael Salomon

Screenplay: Robert Caswell, Jonathan Hensleigh, and Sally Robinson, from the books *A Story Like the Wind* and *A Far Off Place* by Laurens Van der Post. Cinematography by Juan Ruiz-Anchia. 100 minutes

Jack the Bear

Reese Witherspoon (Karen Morris), Danny DeVito, Gary Sinese, Julia Louis-Dreyfus

20th Century Fox/American Filmworks/Lucky Dog Productions, Inc.

Producer: Bruce Gilbert

Director: Marshall Herskovitz

Screenplay: Steven Zaillian, from the novel by Dan McCall. Cinematography by Fred Murphy. 99 minutes

1994
S.F.W.

Reese Witherspoon (Wendy Pfister), Stephen Dorff, Jake Busey, Joey Lauren Adams

A&M Films/PolyGram Filmed Entertainment/Propaganda Films

Producer: Dale Pollock

Director: Jefery Levy

Screenplay: Danny Rubin and Jefery Levy, from the novel by Andrew Wellman. Cinematography by Peter Deming. 96 minutes

1996
Freeway

Reese Witherspoon (Vanessa Lutz), Kiefer Sutherland, Wolfgang Bodison, Dan Hedaya, Brooke Shields

August Entertainment/Davis-Films/Illusion Entertainment/ Kushner-Locke Company/Muse Productions

Producers: Chris Hanley and Brad Wyman

Director: Matthew Bright

Screenplay: Matthew Bright. Cinematography by John Thomas. 110 minutes

Fear

Reese Witherspoon (Nicole Walker), Mark Wahlberg, William Peterson, Amy Brenneman, Alyssa Milano

Imagine Entertainment/Universal Pictures

Producers: Brian Grazer, Ric Kidney, and Karen Snow

Director: James Foley

Screenplay: Christopher Crowe. Cinematography by Thomas Kloss. 97 minutes

1998

Twilight

Reese Witherspoon (Mel Ames), Paul Newman, Susan Sarandon, Gene Hackman, Stockard Channing, James Garner

Cinehaus/ Paramount Pictures/Scott Rudin Productions

Producers: Arlene Donovan and Scott Rudin

Director: Robert Benton

Screenplay: Robert Benton and Richard Russo. Cinematography by Piotr Sobocinski. 94 minutes

Overnight Delivery

Reese Witherspoon (Ivy Miller), Paul Rudd, Christine Taylor, Sarah Silverman

Motion Picture Corporation of America

Producers: Dan Etheridge, Brad Krevoy, and Steven Stabler

Director: Jason Bloom

Screenplay: Marc Sedaka and Steven Bloom. Cinematography by Edward J. Pei. 87 minutes

Pleasantville

Reese Witherspoon (Jennifer), Tobey Maguire, William H. Macy, Joan Allen, Jeff Daniels, Don Knotts

Larger Than Life Productions/New Line Cinema

Producers: Robert J. Degus, Jon Kilik, Gary Ross, and Steven Soderbergh

Director: Gary Ross

Screenplay: Gary Ross. Cinematography by John Lindley. 124 minutes

1999

Cruel Intentions

Reese Witherspoon (Annette Hargrove), Sarah Michelle Gellar, Ryan Phillippe, Selma Blair

Columbia Pictures/Cruel Productions/ Newmarket Capital Group/ Original Film

Producer: Neal H. Moritz

Director: Roger Kumble

Screenplay: Roger Kumble, from the novel *Les liaisons dangereuses* by Choderlos de Laclos. Cinematography by Theo van de Sande. 97 minutes

Election

Reese Witherspoon (Tracy Flick), Matthew Broderick, Chris Klein, Jessica Campbell

Bona Fide Productions/MTV Films/Paramount Pictures

Producers: Albert Berger, David Gale, Keith Samples, and Ron Yerxa
Director: Alexander Payne
Screenplay: Alexander Payne and Jim Taylor, from the novel by Tom
  Perrotta. Cinematography by James Glennon. 103 minutes

Best Laid Plans

Reese Witherspoon (Lissa), Alessandro Nivola, Josh Brolin, Gene
  Wolande
Dogstar Films/Fox 2000 Pictures
Producers: Sean Bailey, Betsy Beers, Alan Greenspan, and Chris Moore
Director: Mike Barker
Screenplay: Ted Griffin. Cinematography by Ben Seresin. 92 minutes

2000

American Psycho

Reese Witherspoon (Evelyn Williams), Christian Bale, Justin Theroux,
  Josh Lucas, Chloë Sevigny
Edward R. Pressman Film Corporation/Lions Gate Films/Muse
  Productions/P.P.S. Films/Quadra Entertainment/Universal
  Pictures
Producers: Christian Halsey Solomon, Chris Hanley, and Edward R.
  Pressman
Director: Mary Harron
Screenplay: Mary Harron and Guinevere Turner, from the novel by
  Bret Easton Ellis. Cinematography by Andrzej Sekula. 101 minutes

Little Nicky

Reese Witherspoon (Angel Holly), Adam Sandler, Patricia Arquette,
  Harvey Keitel, Rodney Dangerfield

Avery Pix/Happy Madison Productions/New Line Cinema/RSC
  Media/The Robert Simonds Company/Robert Simonds Productions
Producers: Jack Giarraputo and Robert Simonds
Director: Steven Brill
Screenplay: Tim Herlihy, Adam Sandler, and Steven Brill. Cinematog-
  raphy by Theo van de Sande. 90 minutes

2001
The Trumpet of the Swan
Reese Witherspoon (voice of Serena), Jason Alexander, Mary Steen-
  burgen, Seth Green, Carol Burnett
Rich-Crest Animation
Producers: Paul J. Newman and Lin Oliver
Directors: Terry L. Noss and Richard Rich
Screenplay: Judy Rothman Rofé, from the book by E. B. White.
  75 minutes. Animated

Legally Blonde
Reese Witherspoon (Elle Woods), Luke Wilson, Selma Blair, Victor
  Garber, Matthew Davis
Marc Platt Productions/MGM
Producers: Ric Kidney and Marc Platt
Director: Robert Luketic
Screenplay: Karen McCullah Lutz and Kirsten Smith, from the novel by
  Amanda Brown. Cinematography by Anthony B. Richmond. 96 minutes

2002
The Importance of Being Earnest
Reese Witherspoon (Cecily), Rupert Everett, Colin Firth, Frances
  O'Connor, Judi Dench

Miramax Films/Ealing Studios/Film Council/Newmarket Capital
Group/Fragile Films
Producer: Barnaby Thompson
Director: Oliver Parker
Screenplay: Oliver Parker, from the play by Oscar Wilde. Cinematography by Tony Pierce-Roberts. 97 minutes

Sweet Home Alabama
Reese Witherspoon (Melanie Smooter), Josh Lucas, Patrick Dempsey, Candice Bergen
D&D Films/Original Film/Pigeon Creek Films/Touchstone Pictures
Producers: Stokely Chaffin and Neal H. Moritz
Director: Andy Tennant
Screenplay: C. Jay Cox, from the story by Douglas J. Eboch. Cinematography by Andrew Dunn. 108 minutes

2003
Legally Blonde 2: Red, White and Blonde
Reese Witherspoon (Elle Woods), Luke Wilson, Sally Field, Regina King
Producers: David Nicksay and Marc Platt
Director: Charles Herman-Wurmfeld
Screenplay: Kate Kondell, from the story by Eve Ahlert, Dennis Drake, and Kate Kondell. Based on characters created by Amanda Brown. Cinematography by Elliot Davis. 95 minutes

2004
Vanity Fair
Reese Witherspoon (Becky Sharp), Gabriel Byrne, James Purefoy, Jim Broadbent, Bob Hoskins

Focus   Features/Granada   Film   Productions/Epsilon   Motion
    Pictures/Tempesta Films
Producers: Janette Day, Lydia Dean Pilcher, and Donna Gigliotti
Director: Mira Nair
Screenplay: Matthew Faulk, Mark Skeet, and Julian Fellowes, from the
    novel by William Makepeace Thackeray. Cinematography by
    Declan Quinn. 141 minutes

2005
Walk the Line
Reese Witherspoon (June Carter), Joaquin Phoenix, Ginnifer
    Goodwin, Robert Patrick
Fox 2000 Pictures/Tree Line Films/Konrad Pictures/Catfish
    Productions
Producers: James Keach and Cathy Konrad
Director: James Mangold
Screenplay: Gill Dennis and James Mangold, from the book *Man in
    Black* by Johnny Cash and *Cash: The Autobiography* by Johnny Cash
    and Patrick Carr. Cinematography by Phedon Papamichael.
    136 minutes

Just Like Heaven
Reese Witherspoon (Elizabeth Masterson), Mark Ruffalo, Donal
    Logue
DreamWorks SKG/MacDonald-Parkes Productions
Producers: Laurie MacDonald and Walter F. Parkes
Director: Mark Waters
Screenplay: Peter Tolan and Leslie Dixon. Cinematography by Daryn
    Okada. 95 minutes

2006
Penelope

Reese Witherspoon (Annie), Christina Ricci, James McAvoy, Catherine O'Hara, Peter Dinklage

Stone Village Pictures/Type A Films/Grosvenor Park Productions/ Tatira/Zephyr Films Ltd.

Producers: Dylan Russell, Jennifer Simpson, Scott Steindorff, and Reese Witherspoon

Director: Mark Palansky

Screenplay: Leslie Caveny. Cinematography by Michel Amathieu. 101 minutes

TELEVISION APPEARANCES

1991
Wildflower

Reese Witherspoon (Ellie Perkins), Beau Bridges, Susan Blakely, William McNamara, Patricia Arquette

Carroll Newman Productions/Freed-Laufer Productions/The Polone Company

Producer: Carroll Newman Executive Producers: Richard Freed, Ira E. Laufer, and Carroll Newman

Director: Diane Keaton

Teleplay: Sara Flanigan, from the book *Alice* by Sara Flanigan. Cinematography by Janusz Kaminski. 120 minutes

1992
Desperate Choices: To Save My Child

Reese Witherspoon (Cassie Robbins), Joanna Kerns, Bruce Davison, Joseph Mazzello, Jeremy Sisto

Executive Producer: Andrew Adelson

Director: Andy Tennant

Teleplay: Sandra Jennings and Maggie Kleinman, from a story by
Sandra Jennings. Cinematography by Peter Stein. 100 minutes

1993

Return to Lonesome Dove

Reese Witherspoon (Ferris Dunnigan), Jon Voight, Barbara Hershey,
Rick Schroder, Louis Gossett Jr., Dennis Haysbert

Producer: Dyson Lovell

Executive Producer: Robert Halmi Jr.

Director: Mike Robe

Teleplay: John Wilder. 322 minutes

2000

Friends

Episode: "The One with Rachel's Sister"

Reese Witherspoon (Jill), Jennifer Aniston, Courteney Cox, Lisa
Kudrow, Matt LeBlanc, Matthew Perry, David Schwimmer

Warner Bros. Television

Producers: Sherry Bilsing, Wendy Knoller, Gigi McCreery, Ellen
Plummer, and Perry Rein

Executive Producers: Kevin Bright, Adam Chase, David Crane, Shana
Goldberg-Meehan, Marta Kauffman, Greg Malins, Seth Kurland,
and Scott Silveri

Director: Gary Halvorson

Teleplay: Sherry Bilsing and Ellen Plummer, story by Seth Kurland. 22
minutes

Friends

Episode: "The One Where Chandler Can't Cry"

Reese Witherspoon (Jill), Jennifer Aniston, Courteney Cox, Lisa Kudrow, Matt LeBlanc, Matthew Perry, David Schwimmer

Warner Bros. Television

Producers: Sherry Bilsing, Wendy Knoller, Gigi McCreery, Jamie O'Connor, Ellen Plummer, and Perry Rein

Executive Producers: Kevin Bright, Adam Chase, David Crane, Shana Goldberg-Meehan, Marta Kauffman, Greg Malins, Seth Kurland, and Scott Silveri

Director: Kevin Bright

Teleplay: Andrew Reich and Ted Cohen. 22 minutes

King of the Hill

Episode: "Hanky Panky: Part 1"

Reese Witherspoon (voice of Debbie), Mike Judge, Kathy Najimy, Pamela Adlon, Brittany Murphy

Series Producers: Kit Boss, Joe Boucher, Greg Cohen, Sivert Glarum, Alex Gregory, Johnny Hardwick, Norm Hiscock, Peter Huyck, Michael Jamin, Paul Lieberstein, Richard Raynis, Garland Testa, and Dean Young

Series Executive Producers: Jonathan Aibel, John Altschuler, Richard Appel, Glenn Berger, Greg Daniels, Mike Judge, Howard Klein, Dave Krinsky, Phil Roman, and Michael Rotenberg

Director: Jeff Myers

Teleplay: Jim Dauterive

King of the Hill

Episode: "Hanky Panky: Part 2"

Reese Witherspoon (voice of Debbie), Mike Judge, Kathy Najimy, Pamela Adlon

Series Producers: Kit Boss, Joe Boucher, Greg Cohen, Sivert Glarum, Alex Gregory, Johnny Hardwick, Norm Hiscock, Peter Huyck,

Michael Jamin, Paul Lieberstein, Richard Raynis, Garland Testa, and Dean Young

Series Executive Producers: Jonathan Aibel, John Altschuler, Richard Appel, Glenn Berger, Greg Daniels, Mike Judge, Howard Klein, Dave Krinsky, Phil Roman, and Michael Rotenberg

Director: Adam Kuhlman

Teleplay: Alan R. Cohen and Alan Freedland

2002

The Simpsons

Episode: "The Bart Wants What It Wants"

Reese Witherspoon (voice of Greta Wolfcastle), Dan Castellaneta, Julie Kavner, Nancy Cartwright, Yeardley Smith, Hank Azaria

Series Producers: Richard Appel, Joseph A. Boucher, Donick Cary, Joel H. Cohen, Jonathan Collier, Greg Daniels, Larry Doyle, John Frink, Tom Gammill, Dan Greaney, Ron Hauge, Ken Keeler, Colin A. B. V. Lewis, Tim Long, Jeff Martin, Tom Martin, Ian Maxtone-Graham, Dan McGrath, George Meyer, David Mirkin, Bill Oakley, Carolyn Omine, Don Payne, Bonita Pietila, Michael Price, Max Pross, Richard Raynis, Jace Richdale, David Sacks, Bill Schultz, Brian Scully, Mike Scully, David Silverman, Denise Sirkot, John Swartzwelder, Julie Thacker, Jon Vitti, Josh Weinstein, and Michael Wolf

Series Executive Producers: David S. Cohen, Gabor Csupo, George Meyer, Bill Oakley, Steve Tompkins, and Josh Weinstein

Director: Michael Polcino

Teleplay: John Frink and Don Payne

Awards and Honors

Academy Awards

2006: Won, Best Performance by an Actress in a Leading Role for *Walk the Line* (2005)

American Comedy Awards

2001: Nominated, Funniest Female Guest Appearance in a TV Series for *Friends* (2000)

2000: Nominated, Funniest Actress in a Motion Picture (Leading Role) for *Election* (1999)

Austin Film Critics Association

2006: Won, Best Actress for *Walk the Line* (2005)

BAFTA Awards

2006: Won, Best Performance by an Actress in a Leading Role for *Walk the Line* (2005)

Blockbuster Entertainment Awards

2000: Won, Favorite Supporting Actress—Drama/Romance for *Cruel Intentions* (1999)

Boston Society of Film Critics Awards

2005: Won, Best Actress for *Walk the Line* (2005)

Broadcast Film Critics Association Awards

2006: Won, Best Actress for *Walk the Line* (2005)

Chicago Film Critics Association Awards

2000: Nominated, Best Actress for *Election* (1999)

Cognac Festival du Film Policier

1997: Won, Best Actress for *Freeway* (1996)

Florida Film Critics Circle Awards

2005: Won, Best Actress for *Walk the Line* (2005)

Golden Globes

2006: Won, Best Performance by an Actress in a Motion Picture—Musical or Comedy for *Walk the Line* (2005)

2002: Nominated, Best Performance by an Actress in a Motion Picture—Musical or Comedy for *Legally Blonde* (2001)

2000: Nominated, Best Performance by an Actress in a Motion Picture—Musical or Comedy for *Election* (1999)

Independent Spirit Awards

2000: Nominated, Best Female Lead for *Election* (1999)

Kansas City Film Critics Circle Awards

2006: Won, Best Actress for *Walk the Line* (2005)

2000: Won, Best Actress for *Election* (1999)

Kids' Choice Awards

2002: Nominated, Blimp Award, Favorite Female Movie Star for *Legally Blonde* (2001)

Las Vegas Film Critics Society Sierra Awards

2005: Won, Best Actress for *Walk the Line* (2005)

2000: Nominated, Best Actress for *Election* (1999)

MTV Movie Awards, USA

2006: Nominated, Best Female Performance for *Walk the Line* (2005)

2003: Nominated, Best Female Performance for *Sweet Home Alabama* (2002)

2002: Won, Best Comedic Performance for *Legally Blonde* (2001)

2002: Won, Best Dressed for *Legally Blonde* (2001)

2002: Won, Best Line for *Legally Blonde* (2001)—"Oh, I like your outfit, too; except when I dress up as a frigid bitch, I try not to look so constipated."

2002: Nominated, Best Female Performance for *Legally Blonde* (2001)

MTV Movie Awards, Mexico

2004: Nominated, Best Look (*Mejor Look*) for *Legally Blonde 2: Red, White and Blonde* (2003)

National Society of Film Critics Awards

2006: Won, Best Actress for *Walk the Line* (2005)

2000: Won, Best Actress for *Election* (1999)

New York Film Critics Circle Awards

2005: Won, Best Actress for *Walk the Line* (2005)

Online Film Critics Society Awards

2006: Won, Best Actress for *Walk the Line* (2005)

2000: Won, Best Actress for *Election* (1999)

People's Choice Awards

2006: Won, Favorite Leading Lady

2005: Nominated, Favorite Female Movie Star

San Francisco Film Critics Circle

2005: Won, Best Actress for *Walk the Line* (2005)

Satellite Awards

2005: Won, Outstanding Actress in a Motion Picture, Comedy or Musical for *Walk the Line* (2005)

2002: Nominated, Best Performance by an Actress in a Motion Picture, Comedy or Musical for *Legally Blonde* (2001)

2000: Nominated, Best Performance by an Actress in a Motion Picture, Comedy or Musical for *Election* (1999)

Screen Actors Guild Awards

2006: Won, Outstanding Performance by a Female Actor in a Leading Role for *Walk the Line* (2005)

Sitges—Catalonian International Film Festival

1997: Won, Best Actress for *Freeway* (1997)

Teen Choice Awards

2006: Won, Choice Movie Actress: Drama/Action Adventure for *Walk the Line* (2005)

2003: Won, Choice Movie Liplock for *Sweet Home Alabama* (2002) (shared with Josh Lucas)

2003: Nominated, Choice Movie Actress: Comedy for *Sweet Home Alabama* (2002)

2002: Won, Extraordinary Achievement Award

2002: Nominated, Choice Movie Actress: Comedy for *The Importance of Being Earnest* (2002)

1999: Nominated, Choice Movie Actress for *Cruel Intentions* (1999)

1999: Nominated, Choice Movie Hissy Fit for *Election* (1999)

1999: Nominated, Sexiest Movie Love Scene for *Cruel Intentions* (1999) (shared with Ryan Phillippe)

Washington, D.C., Area Film Critics Association Awards

2005: Won, Best Actress for *Walk the Line* (2005)

Young Artist Awards

1994: Won, Best Youth Actress Costarring in a Motion Picture Drama for *Jack the Bear* (1993)

1993: Nominated, Best Young Actress in a Television Movie for *Desperate Choices: To Save My Child* (1992)

1992: Nominated, Best Young Actress Starring in a Motion Picture for *The Man in the Moon* (1991)

Young Hollywood Awards

1999: Won, Breakthrough Performance—Female for *Pleasantville* (1998)

About the Author

Lauren Brown is an accomplished writer and pop culture fanatic. She began a career on the entertainment path as an intern at *Rolling Stone*. After graduating from the University of South Florida in 1999, Lauren moved to New York City, where she worked at *CosmoGIRL!* as entertainment editor. From there she worked at *Us Weekly* and *Inside TV* magazines. Currently, Lauren is a producer at Sirius Satellite Radio. Throughout her career, Lauren has interviewed a wide array of popular celebrities, including Jessica Simpson, Ashton Kutcher, Luke Wilson, Matthew McConaughey, Anne Hathaway, Steven Tyler, and Kirsten Dunst. Lauren is also the author of *Lindsay Lohan: The It Girl Next Door* and *Emma Roberts: Simply Fabulous*. She currently resides in Manhattan.